Soul in Control

Reflections of a Reformed
Superwoman

Janet M. Neal

BALBOA.
PRESS
A DIVISION OF HAY HOUSE

ISBN: 978-1-4525-5155-5 (sc)
ISBN: 978-1-4525-5156-2 (e)

Library of Congress Control Number: 2012938887

Balboa Press books may be ordered through booksellers or by contacting:

Balboa Press
A Division of Hay House
1663 Liberty Drive
Bloomington, IN 47403
www.balboapress.com
1-(877) 407-4847

Because of the dynamic nature of the Internet, any web addresses or links contained in this book may have changed since publication and may no longer be valid. The views expressed in this work are solely those of the author and do not necessarily reflect the views of the publisher, and the publisher hereby disclaims any responsibility for them.

The author of this book does not dispense medical advice or prescribe the use of any technique as a form of treatment for physical, emotional, or medical problems without the advice of a physician, either directly or indirectly. The intent of the author is only to offer information of a general nature to help you in your quest for emotional and spiritual well-being. In the event you use any of the information in this book for yourself, which is your constitutional right, the author and the publisher assume no responsibility for your actions.

Cover Design by Marie Lourdes.

Printed in the United States of America

Balboa Press rev. date: 08/06/2012

To my three beautiful children, who teach me, inspire me and create the love and laughter in my heart.

When we forget what we should be,
We find who we are

Contents

Introduction

IT WAS THE HAIR gel that woke me up. Up until then, I was able to dismiss the other blunders, barely acknowledging the pattern that was emerging. But as that extra firm hair gel started to grip and hold, it got my attention. Even though I had used it daily for weeks, I had never really appreciated its strength before. Not until the day I applied it…to my face.

Sure, I had a lot on my plate. Who doesn't? Selling a house, buying a new one. Juggling home, work, a new puppy, and a new relationship. It was all just more, more, more. The balls were still being juggled effectively and I was getting by. Or so I thought. It was really the application of hair gel to my face that finally made me wake up.

Earlier in the week, in the midst of the angst of home selling and contemplating the next steps in my business, I received an e-mail which essentially shook me up and started the unraveling of my very loosely held together life. It seemed that the newsletter I had been publishing for the past six years had a title that was "owned" by another person. This fact was brought to my attention through an e-mail encouraging me to cease and desist any and all use of the name. In truth, this was not a big deal – except to me. That name was part of my identity and work of which I was proud. The e-mail served to unleash a plethora of emotions that I had buried while attending to my very busy life and left me feeling frustrated and angry, with a huge resentment that I was not willing to release.

I planned, and schemed, and ran through a vast number of scenarios ranging from downright evil to Zen-like magnificent. My righteous indignation ran amok. And that was not all that ran amok. In one day I sent two e-mail introductions to the wrong people: Raymond received the one intended for Randee and Karla R. received Karla L.'s instead. Now, instead of the name of a placement firm, the recipient got the name of a pizza place, and instead of an entrepreneur, they got an executive. A cosmic mismatch. Then I received a call from my insurance agent who was wondering what happened to my monthly payment. I knew I had sent it electronically. It was later in the day that I received the thank you from Sears for the unexpected, unnecessary payment, which of course should have gone to State Farm. And then I put the hair gel on my face.

As the gel hardened and shocked me back to the here and now, it literally made me stop and look at myself in the mirror. I was forced to slow down and face the fact that I was feeling no longer in control of the many moving pieces of my life. Doing everything by myself just wasn't working. Something needed to change. I flashed on the story of the Buddhist monks and the woman at the stream:

Two monks were traveling together when they came to a river with a strong current. As the monks were preparing to cross the river, they saw a very young and beautiful woman also attempting to cross. The young woman asked the monks if they could help her.

The younger of the two monks hesitated as they were not supposed to have any physical contact with women. The older monk gently motioned the woman onto his back and proceeded to help the woman across the river. Upon reaching the other bank of the river, the woman got down, thanked the monks and went away.

As the monks continued their journey, the younger monk became increasingly agitated and finally spoke out, "Brother, you know we are not permitted to have any contact with women, how could you carry that woman on your shoulders?"

The older monk looked at him and softly replied, "You are right, I did carry that woman. But I have already put her down many hours ago after we crossed the river. Why are you still carrying her?"

I realized that I was carrying a whole mountain of things with me – to do lists from the present, expectations for the future, burdens from the past – and the magnitude of it was clouding my vision, my thoughts, and my ability to function effectively. One by one I had to acknowledge, and let go of, angers, resentments, perceptions and opinions that were doing nothing but weighing me down and misdirecting my life. High on my "items to release" list was the newsletter. With an acknowledgment of what was right, a release of my pride, and through a synchronistic conversation with a friend, I let go of the old newsletter name and welcomed in the new version: *A Balanced Perspective*.

This book is a compilation of articles written during my journey in going from living a controlled life that was led by my ego, my mind and my thoughts, to leading a life of grace and ease, where I invite my Soul to be in control. Think of this book as your karmic wake-up call. If that doesn't work, a little extra firm hair gel on the face may do the trick!

Chapter One

Becoming Aware

The Chair Incident

I HATE BEING EARLY. Being on time even brings its own set of anxiety for me, but early? Downright nearly puts me over the edge. Last week I showed up early to a meeting and sure enough, was presented with not one, but two anxiety provoking scenarios: 1) having to make small talk with someone I didn't know very well, and 2) picking a place to sit. This proved to be the more difficult scenario. Not only did placement come into the equation (not too close, not too far), but there were a variety of chair types from which to choose. Did I want one with arms, or without? Cushions or no cushions? Straight back or slightly slanted? Seriously, WAY too many choices! I realized that I could: a) stand there all day and worry about it; b) wait until the room filled up and take what was left; or c) just go with what seemed right at that moment and hope for the best. I chose the latter.

As I sat and waited for the meeting to begin (and stewed at being there so very early!), I realized that this "chair incident" was such a metaphor for my life right now. A month or so ago I was given a workbook to fill with my goals for the year. Being a goal-driven person, I knew it was a good activity – until I actually had to put them on paper. It was like walking into that room and seeing all those chairs. Where to start? Which one to pick? The choices become overwhelming. And just like my choices with the chairs, my choices in life come down to either spending my time worrying about them, waiting until life or someone else forces my decisions, or just going with what feels right at the time and hoping for the best. Gulp. Pretty tough stuff for someone who traditionally has been concerned about making sure she is doing the "right" thing, and doing it perfectly as well.

I keep thinking about Mark Zuckerberg and Facebook. I haven't seen the movie yet, but I get the impression that he started Facebook to meet girls. I don't think he set out to create something that would one day create a platform that could rally millions to peacefully topple a corrupt government. Meeting girls – doable. Overthrowing governments – yeah, not so sure. But he just chose what was in front of him, what felt right at the time. He took action. There was no way he could have had any concept of his actions' unbelievable consequences.

So, for today, I'll show up. Maybe not on time. Definitely not early. But I'll take a deep breath and keep moving. Hey, you never know where this path may lead me.

Selflessly Selfish

I WANT WHAT I want when I want it. So basically I guess you could say that I am selfish. However, there are also many times (decades, actually) where everyone else's needs/opinions/desires came before mine. In other words, I'm a selfless selfish person.

As you can imagine this personality contradiction has caused a great deal of internal conflict. Perhaps it is why I was always a middle-of-the-road kind of person most of my life – too complicated to choose one side or the other. Compromise may be the name of the game, but as you may imagine, this is not an easy solution for either side of my persona. My selfish side doesn't want to give any ground and my selfless side feels guilty and unworthy of doing the same. It's a Freudian conundrum.

I've had to make decisions in the past which strongly invoke this schizoid personality. Whether it is for a career decision or a relationship issue, the result is the same: I am frustrated regardless of the outcome. I do black and white – I don't do gray easily. Perhaps this is just another reason I abhor most of the winter months: they are SO gray. With the exception of my hair, gray is definitely not my favorite color.

I am working hard to be comfortable with being uncomfortable. In some ways, it is one of the hardest things I've ever attempted to do. Going through life without knowing all the answers – or risking that someone may actually notice that I don't – is a bit unnerving. And yet, the mere act of being vulnerable serves not only to bring me out of my selfishness, but releases me from the people-pleasing selflessness.

I'm taking a deep breath on that one. Here goes nothing…

Making it Fit

As I WADED THROUGH the widely strewn contents of my basement in preparation for moving, I muttered more than a few choice comments about my ex-husband's purchasing habits regarding home improvement project materials. We owned more "make your own screen" kits than we had windows in our house. And just how many new door latches does one REALLY need? I was feeling very smug – until I got to the home office/study area and found my Achilles heel: office and school supplies. At last count I have unearthed 11 unopened sets of divider tabs, probably 40 folders, and possibly 20 notebooks. Let's not even talk about the pens, pencils and paper of various stock, color and usage. And there still are three unexplored boxes just waiting to expose my weakness.

OK, so I've uncovered another hidden treasure of moving – the exposure to all your "stuff." Not only am I finding physical stuff that I had long forgotten, but I am finding all sorts of goodies of the emotional nature. One of these more interesting "finds" is my need to categorize.

Any good organizer worth his or her salt gleefully will charge you with the painful, yet necessary task, of deciding what stays and what goes. That is phase one. Next, lump together those things which share some common component or usage. This task I actually find very rewarding. I now actually can find kitchen items easily, the kids can, at a glance, find the Xbox game vs. the Playstation ones, and, of course, there are those office supplies. The problem is what to do with the stuff that doesn't fit neatly into a category or group. For example: what do I do with the baby books? Are they to be shelved with the photos, or archived with the "we won't need these for a long time" items? They could go either way.

Which begs the much deeper question: what do I do with the other things in my life which I can't categorize?

My career had been put pretty much on hold as I was consumed with this move. As I see the light at the end of the tunnel of boxes, I realize it is time for me to start making some decisions. But how to categorize them? How do you reinvent your reinvented self? Which parts do you keep, which do you throw away, and what do you do with the stuff that doesn't fit neatly in one compartment?

I realized that the process is the same as the one I have been using for wading through my physical stuff:

Step one: Make a list of what I need.

Step Two: Be willing to let go of that which is not necessary or no longer relevant.

Step Three: Take an inventory of that which remains and give it the "gut test:" Imagine my life with it and feel the feeling I get from keeping it. Then imagine my life without it and notice that feeling. The gut never lies...

Step Four: Put aside that which doesn't make sense right now. Revisit it in a week, or a month. It may have found its home by then, or at least a clearer answer.

Step Five: Step back and look at what I've got. Make any minor adjustments.

Step Six: Celebrate the new me!

I'm coming to realize that life is not about what compartment you fit in or even if you spill over into a couple along the way. Life is a series of readjustments, a response to continual internal and external changes. And really, as long as you know where the important stuff is, what else do you need? But if you need office supplies, give me a call...

Leftovers

I DON'T KNOW WHAT is more stuffed with turkey, dressing and pie – me or my refrigerator. As I gaze at its contents, now overflowing with bits and pieces of a wonderful holiday celebration, I can't help but wonder what truly makes the Thanksgiving leftovers so great: their flavor, or their memories. A bite of the turkey reminds me of the oft-repeated "just 20 more minutes" before the bird was ready. The aroma of the sweet potato casserole elicits a smirk as I remember the forced smile I wore when its contents were described to me – and my subsequent sheepish request for seconds after my hesitant initial taste test proved a delightful surprise. And the melt-in-your-mouth sweetness of the apple pie warms my heart with the memory of love and appreciation at my handiwork.

Since when did leftovers get such a good rap?

Wasn't there a time, not so long ago, when I myself felt like a "leftover?" A remnant of a past life – incomplete, worked over, and left on a shelf for another day? A walk around my house was a tour of a life that use to be: half the crystal, a few snatched wrenches from a toolbox, books with no book shelf, chairs with no table, empty spots where family portraits use to hang.

When you are viewing life through the lens of "less than", then life takes on that negative hue. You notice what you don't have and find evidence of it everywhere. Just like when you're looking for a car and that is the only car you see on the road, or when you're trying to get pregnant and all you see are babies, or you're divorced and all you see are happy looking families everywhere. Leftover is what happens when you don't have the complete picture.

Thanksgiving, however, has made me realize that there is yet a different way to look at leftovers. Rather than focusing on what is missing, focus on what is present. Yes, there may not be enough fine china left for a party of eight, but hey, there's plenty for an intimate dinner party. And the food not consumed at this meal will provide the basis for future meals which bring their own memories. That which is left is often more flavorful, as the individual ingredients have had time to age and integrate thoroughly into a new, more robust version of themselves. And life, as a leftover, is equally as rich: embroidered with the trappings and trimmings of days gone by and poised to take advantage of the moment present.

If life were such that I had a choice to start afresh, or to move forward with the collection of experiences that I've accumulated, there would be no hesitation in my choosing. I would gather up my bags of leftovers, grateful for each morsel, and head on down that winding road. What was once thought of as a burden, now has become a life-sustainer and enhancer. Life as a leftover brings new hope, new experiences for growth and new ways to transform that which was, into that which will be – and it's pretty darn tasty too!

Ode to Ralph Nader

BACK WHEN THE "GREEN Movement" was known as "Ecology" and when "rapping" was not something accompanied by a beat, I was a Midwestern girl with intentions to change the world. So it was not surprising that, when Ralph Nader came to my college campus, I was one of the first in line to see him. His visit came shortly after he had caused the stir that created seat belts and his youthful, anti-establishment, "power to the people" message stirred my own social activism. A picture from the front page of the college newspaper shows him speaking to a rapt audience – with me in the front row, pigtailed and bell-bottomed, sitting cross-legged on the gym floor, gazing intently at him. Truly a moment of inspiration.

However, the truth of the situation was that if you looked again at the picture, there is a gorgeous guy sitting next to me named Jeff Carr, whom I had been wanting to get to know, and I spent the entire lecture thinking about how cool it was that he was next to me, that we could talk about it on the way out, that this would be the beginning a beautiful relationship, how cute our kids would be.... I have no idea what Ralph Nader said.

So, when the opportunity came to go hear Ralph Nader, a couple of decades later, I jumped on it. Assured that there would be no Jeff Carr to distract me, I was eager to hear Nader's message on social entrepreneurship. And he did not disappoint. Outside of a few curmudgeonly statements, like, "What is this obsession with music?!" he remains an inspiration to "just do it." It is more than a little humbling to look at what I have accomplished over the past 40 years, versus his list.

His message conveyed a sense of urgency, that time is a wasting, people. He expressed his frustration with society and how the "trivialization of time is staggering." We cannot afford to act as if we have all the time in the world to solve our problems, for if we refuse to act, our days could indeed be numbered.

I left there pumped up and ready for the fight. The only problem is, fighting for what? Days before I had been in a state of perpetual frustration over trying to figure out what was next for me and had just come to the acceptance that time takes time. This was going to be a process and I needed to allow it to unfold. Now I was feeling that urgency again. I had the fuel, but where was the vehicle?

I wish I could say that I have since found the answer and am charging down my path. What is interesting, though, is that maybe I am and I don't even know it. One of my favorite authors, Kent Nerburn, in his book *Simple Truths,* talks about it being the small touches that become our legacy to the universe. He says, "If we have played our part well, offering love where it was needed, strength and caring where it was lacking; if we tended the earth and its creatures with a sense of humble stewardship, we will have done enough."

Maybe I am not destined to be a Ralph Nader and have a resume of accomplishments that far exceed the recommended one to two pages. Maybe my work will not cure the ills of many or cause social change in the world. Maybe my path is a simpler one, but still important in the grand schemes of the universe none the less.

I may not ever know how my life touches another, but I do know how others touch me. And so thank you to all of you who have, in your own ways, shaped my life to be what it is today. And thank you, Ralph Nader, for your inspiration, vision, and continued message of social activism. That and for letting me meet Jeff Carr.

Hidden in Plain Sight

A RIDDLE FOR YOU: What can be both seen and unseen at the same time?

Answer: The Truth

It is easy to see the answer when it is about someone else and yet can be invisible, at the same time, to one's own self. Boggles the mind. This principle became very clear to me last week when my son was berating me for not paying more attention to our older dog. He said, "Just because the puppy demands your attention and makes it difficult to spend any time with the other dog, it is just not right or fair to the older dog." I just stared at him in amazement because he was describing the scenario between himself and his younger siblings. It was amazing to me that he could see the phenomenon very clearly in another context but was totally clueless when I asked him if he saw any parallels to his life. It reminded me of a friend who will talk about how someone is so nasty and biased – and then, in almost the same sentence, will exhibit nearly the same traits. I have been left speechless on more than one occasion by the irony of it.

Lest I seem all high and mighty about this, it occurred to me this morning that if others behave this way, then most certainly I must do so as well. For example, I know that I have a blind spot about my fear of making a wrong decision. Somewhere, a long time ago, I came up with the irrational belief that I need to make the RIGHT decision...or else.... This mindset can be crippling and tremendously ineffectual and generally is applied to decisions that have some sort of ego stake attached to it. I will sit on the sidelines for a long time, just observing, before I'll jump in. On the other hand, I have countless examples of times I've made a decision and found out it wasn't a good one... and I've actually lived to talk about it! In fact, most times, I've come out better on the other end *because* of those decisions. And yet I can almost see that in-denial part of me closing its eyes, with hands over the ears and humming madly so as not to hear the truth.

I think I may see next year's New Year's resolution in the making....

Let the Sun Shine

THE OTHER DAY I awoke early and got ready in a dimly lit room, trying not to wake anyone. I kept applying makeup, as it didn't seem to be "taking." By the time I got out into the car and the daylight and looked at myself in the mirror there, the only words that came to mind were, "I'm ready for my close-up now, Mr. DeMille."

I've become someone who is very sensitive to light – not in the sense that I can't bear to be out in it – but more so that I am extremely attuned to it. I will notice if there is a change to anything in the environment, like a tree being removed, which affects the light patterns. I even think of my life in terms of light vs. dark. Being a very visual person, if I "see" a picture of a scene from any particular time in my life, I see it in shades of brightness, depending on the emotional context. I once was trying to explain to a client that his company was a "light" environment for me versus others with whom I had worked. Not so sure he got it, or me, but I know I was at least entertaining to him!

Letting the light into my life, from the literal to the spiritual, has been a transitional process. I was reflecting on how even my choice of housing has been indicative of how much or how little light I was willing to allow into my life. My first apartment was a basement apartment: enough said. I was definitely in a shut down/cocoon stage of my life at that point. I progressed to an attic apartment, but with not much window space there either, and then moved to a place in the woods. Next was an apartment with dark woodwork and did I even open my curtains? Finally, my life started to turn and I lived in houses with big windows that let in lots of light, just as I was allowing light to flow in and out of me.

This summer my goal has been to have a deep tan. I know – very shallow of me! But getting it means I am spending a lot of time outside, soaking up that Vitamin D (with sunscreen, of course), and letting that light just soak on in. It's a nice reminder of the need to be open to that which is around me. And a better one than a Gloria Swanson makeup lesson!

You Can't Go Home Again
(and other good news…)

FOR THE LAST FEW years I've been asking friends what it was like having their college freshman child come home for that first vacation. Invariably I'm greeted with sighs, rolling eyes and then a quick, "Oh, I mean, it's good to see them again…" I think part of me was trying to bolster myself for that inevitable time in my life. I guess I just didn't think it was going to come quite so soon.

I was, basically, a model daughter. I know my sisters are reading this now and either laughing or rolling their eyes. But from a mother's perspective, I was easy – rarely talked back, did as I was told, didn't get in trouble, good student, good friends…the whole nine yards. Then I went off to college. I remember coming home that first time and found it awkwardly uncomfortable – like a familiar pair of pants that now just didn't fit quite right. Here I had been independent all this time and now they were "telling" me what to do?! I had to watch what I said and how I said it. Conversations that before would have seemed meaningful were now woefully unsatisfying. And don't even get me started on their politics! The interesting fact was that my mom actually shared my uncomfortable feeling, but from a different perspective. Of course, knowing that didn't make it any better.

So fast forward to this past weekend. My eldest son, just 16, came home for the first time since going off to his ski academy in September. His brother, sister and I were all excited to be with this new "grown up" version of the one who had left in the fall. And that enthusiasm lasted, oh, about 15 minutes. Then we were right back where we left off, but with a different intensity. It seemed that not only had he changed, but we had too. I was expecting his reaction, but it was interesting to view it this time from the parental viewpoint. And it was also a relief that things weren't exactly the same as they had been a few months before. If they were, then neither one of us would have done any growing.

Change of any kind is uncomfortable. But without it, we stagnate and wither on the vine. Change infers growth of some sort. On my son's part, he now has learned to relate to kids his own age, to establish his own routine, and to claim his independence. On my side of the equation, I am learning to understand what I like and don't like in my environment and am setting clearer boundaries to establish and keep things that way. The other two siblings have been living and evolving with our family's new routines, making it all the more foreign to my son.

We did a bit of "testing the waters," learned what we will accept and what we won't. We argued a bit, but we laughed too. I marveled at how my little boy is no longer little or a boy, but a young man, full of energy and intelligence and humor and personality. And I marveled at myself for giving him the space to grow and yet allowing myself to do the same.

I am really grateful for all the uncomfortable feelings we had this weekend. Thomas Wolfe was right that, "You can't go home again." Not if you and those at home have grown at all. You can fall back into some of the old patterns, you can follow some of the same routines, but it will never be quite the same again. Thank goodness for that – just more evidence that we're moving forward! And as Martha Stewart would say, "It's a good thing!"

The Magic Words: Snow Day

I'VE BEEN SPENDING A lot of time in California – Southern California to be precise. And I am finding it harder and harder to leave the warmth and sun and blue sky and flowers and trees and grass....you get the picture! So you would think that a day like today – a blizzard – would be the final straw to send me straight to the online realtors to start finding my next home. Instead, I'm blissfully content.

It's a "snow day" here. For anyone who grew up in a snowy clime, the mention of that term awakens the jubilant inner child. What could be better than a day that breaks from the "have to's" and allows you to rejoice in the "want to's"? And having been a teacher, I can vouch for the fact that teachers, too, get just as giddy!

What is it about a snow day that is so fabulous? The answer really depends upon your perspective. My children, who normally take at least three reminders to even *think* of leaving the comfort of their beds, BOUNDED out of bed this morning, full of energy. Calls were immediately made to friends to make all-important plans. They have spent the whole day, so far, with smiles on their faces, gliding from activity to activity without any intervention on my part. It's amazing to me how effortless this is for them, considering the countless "I'm bored!" or, "I don't know what to do," statements I have heard from them at other times in their lives! Here's a day for them <u>full</u> of opportunity to do whatever they want. No one telling them what to do and when to do it; no homework, no pressure.

For me, I shut off the alarm and pulled the covers over my head – with a big smile. When I did get out of bed, I proceeded to take my time getting to my computer, resplendent in my PJs and Paul Frank slippers (which I stole from my 11-year-old daughter). Later I worked my way up to dressing in sweats. Life is good…

Years ago when I was in a very stressful time of my life, I was inspired by a snowstorm to write the following poem:

> *Snow is God's swaddling for the earth*
> *it calms*
> *it quiets*
> *it brings serenity and beauty*
> *The snowplows come, kicking off the covers,*
> *releasing the angry and frustrated child*
> *to scream once more.*

Today I wrote to a friend, "Snow days are good for the spirit." They do an amazing job of giving me an "excuse" to slow down and to do what I want to do, without any outside pressures. It feels good – no, it feels GREAT. And it is a wonderful reminder of the necessity of taking the time to slow down, to play, to lounge, to just hang out. No guilt, no pressure. It's the recharge my inner batteries need to keep me going at my often too-busy pace. It's the recharge my mind needs to be able to think more clearly and make better decisions. It's the recharge my spirit needs to reconnect with that which is most important to me.

If I weren't fortunate enough to enjoy an actual "snow day", I think I'd have to create one in my life. I'd pretend that I couldn't go out and run around doing my endless errands. I'd watch those movies I've rented or recorded but never have time to watch. Curl up with a good book. Take a long nap or sleep in. Call a friend or loved one. Be a "human being," not a "human doing" for a day. Life will be there waiting upon my return!

Lessons from Lily

YESTERDAY I WAS IN a silly mood and was doing a very goofy dance in the kitchen, à la Elaine from *Seinfeld*. My daughter, by now resigned to the fact that she has a slightly bizarre mother, said, "Mom, look at the dogs!" I turned around to see my pups looking at me with heads tipped to the side. And the looks on their faces were a mix between sheer horror and disbelief. I was half expecting them to say "What in the WORLD are you doing?!" Rather humbling to be dissed by a dog.

I decided to observe my pets to see what else I could learn from them on the secrets of life. Lily, the year-old pup, lives for walks and attention and Trixie, the 9-year old lump, lives for food and naps. I am in agreement with both lifestyles. But here are the other things I have learned:

- There is no love except unconditional love
- A little affection helps brighten spirits
- Run hard/rest hard
- Make each day an adventure by seeing your surroundings with new eyes
- Protect your loved ones from the "bad guys" and enjoy their friends
- The simplest things bring the greatest pleasure
- Be consistent, hold your boundaries and make sure you praise the good stuff

Lily just came up to check on me as I was writing this. Another lesson: Much can be said without ever uttering a word.

Janet M. Neal

Life is a Walk in the Woods

I WENT FOR A walk in the woods today and I learned a lot more about life. I realized that we are surrounded with examples of how to live our lives. The trees, for instance, have much to teach us.

The first tree I saw was a towering beauty. I was drawn to it by what appeared from a distance to be a hollow interior. As I got closer, I saw that it was, indeed, hollowed, due to a fire at some point its existence. Dark scars covered its exterior, making it stand out from those around it. And yet, here it was, standing tall and proud. It was reaching ever skyward and life poured out of its limbs at the highest levels. I looked around and noticed other trees whose bark had been licked by fire, all still holding strong. The secret, I surmised, was to stay strong, weather adversity, and continue to reach higher.

I then saw another large tree, its bottom limbs covered with moss. As the moss overcame the tree, it had given over part of itself to the growth. It still had its own leafy branches on the top but I wondered how long this would last: A year, a decade, a lifetime? I saw that if you allowed it, something could literally take over your life. The secret, it seemed, was in the balance.

I saw tall trees and short trees. Trees covered in lush leaves, and trees sprouting only a few leaves clinging to a lonely limb. I saw trees that were singular and those rooted together. I found the ones that were the most gnarled, that were the most unique, to be the most beautiful. They stood out, looking proud and wise. Their waning strength gave the forest its character.

Scattered among the living were the remnants of other former tenants, felled by some natural force in days gone by. They lay there, peaceful reminders of perhaps some not-too-peaceful past. They remain among the living, a part of the bigger picture, and playing a new role. They may be dead in the literal sense, but they are full of life, as a home for forest insects, a hideaway for a chipmunk, or a resting spot for a weary traveler. Life goes on, regardless of the form it takes.

My walk through the woods was a gift and an education. I walked slowly, reverently, in the presence of such magnificence. The silence was palpable, the peace and wisdom awe-inspiring. I was humbled to be in their presence, a mere mortal among the wisdom of the ages.

Life, it seems, is full of messages. We are, indeed, given a manual for living if we only look around and notice its lessons. The beauty of life is in the diversity of its components.

There is room for the damaged, the struggling, the weak and the strong. There is a quiet persistence in living, and a dignity in death. The secret is to put down strong roots, stand proud in your uniqueness, and keep reaching for the sky. The rest is just window dressing.

Janet M. Neal

Getting the Real Thing

ONE OF MY FAVORITE playground activities as a kid was playing on the merry-go-round, that circular metal contraption with bars that you used to both push it faster and faster, and also to hang on for dear life. Depending on my mood, I would either be pushing it harder and harder until my little sister was totally freaked out, or wrapping my limbs around the bars, a smile on my face, enjoying the wind in my hair and the feeling of escape. Ah, memories....

I remember vividly how we begged my parents to get our own merry-go-round for our backyard and how absolutely dumbstruck we were when they actually bought one! Of course, true to my family's nature, you couldn't buy the name brand. My mother sewed all our clothing and we grew up brainwashed to think that clothes with labels were just short of evil. When skateboarding became the craze and our neighborhood's "Surf City" was the giant hill at the bottom of our street, we begged for our own equipment. Instead of getting the model that the other kids had, we got a red "Little Dink." It was embarrassing to ride it in public.

So you can imagine our disappointment when my dad put together our new merry-go-round and we found out that instead of a flat surface that you could roll around on and contort your body around the poles to try daring moves, we had something more akin to a "real" merry-go-round: actual seats that all faced in one direction. When I sat on them and was pushed, it made me nauseous. I don't remember going on it more than once.

I know now that my parents did their very best to give us what they could with their limited means. I also have learned that it is important to be specific when asking for something! I admit that there have been times when I was one of those women who felt that if a guy really loved me, he would know what I wanted. That assumption probably works if you're dating a psychic, but it is not effective with most men. And the same thing applies when asking for things in your life in general. Once I made my "List of Intentions" and one of them was, "To be on Oprah." Four months later, as I sat in the audience of *The Oprah Winfrey Show* I realized that I should have indicated, "To be a *guest* on Oprah, on the stage with her." I really had gotten just what I asked for.

Some days when I find myself bemoaning my surroundings, my stuff, my lot in life, I have to stop and realize that perhaps I really <u>have</u> gotten what I've asked for. If I'm focused on the negative, that's what I'll attract. If I focus on abundance, that, too, is what I'll attract. I'm looking for a life that lets me feel the wind in my hair, not one that makes me feel nauseous. I think it's time to start revising my intentions list!

Janet M. Neal

Playing to Your Strengths

I HEARD A STORY recently about a group of animal parents who were looking to start a school for their children. They made sure they had the best of instructors to teach their darling offspring how to be the best runners, jumpers, swimmers, and climbers. The Rabbit family, therefore, was quite dismayed when their little Bunny was placed in a remedial course for both swimming and climbing. Where had they gone wrong? They wallowed in their self-pity for only a moment before they put a new plan in place: tutors, extra practice sessions and possibly researching the credentials of the swimming and climbing instructors. Their little angel would be successful, by hook or by crook!

I must admit, I both laughed and cringed at hearing the story, as it hits a little too close to home! How often in my quest to provide the best possible stimulating, educational and diverse environment and opportunities for my children do I overlook the reality of a situation? How often do I really do this to myself?

Playing to your strengths is not a new concept but one that I think has been overlooked in this highly competitive world. If you look at any work environment, you will find it teeming with people who were so good at their previous jobs that they were promoted – into a new job, which does not take advantage of the experience which made them successful in the first place! And while it is admirable to expand your horizons and enhance your abilities, it should not be done at the expense of your strengths.

I need to learn not to discount my strengths – they are there for a reason. I need to learn to embrace them and utilize them. My strengths are the answer to someone's needs and I need to discover them, celebrate them, and share them with all! And if I can't do everything perfectly, who cares? There is certainly someone else who can pick up the slack.

Taking Life Literally

I AM A GREAT one for jumping to conclusions. I'm always trying to figure out book endings based on the first chapter, finishing my kid's sentences or singing a song based on the first notes. Maybe it's from watching *Jeopardy* all these years and trying to beat the buzzers! Or maybe it is the frenetic pace at which I live my life – I just don't have time to wait for "the rest of the story."

Part of the problem with living your life this way, outside of the obvious miscommunications, is that you tend to take life literally. You draw immediate conclusions based on small bits of information taken as facts. Once the conclusion has been drawn, your actions fall in line.

Life, however, is really more of a metaphor. We continually are given information about what to do. It comes in all forms, from conversations with friends, family or coworkers to that seemingly random thought that pops into our minds. The beauty and subtlety of life reside in the interpretation of this data and how we choose to act upon it.

Let me give you an example. Since I was a little girl, I always have felt that I wanted to become a teacher. I played school with my sisters and friends, volunteered as an aide while in high school and pursued a teaching degree in college. I secured a teaching job and loved it – for about three years. After that, I was burnt out and resigned to pursue life on the corporate side of the fence. Yet I still felt that pull to teach. Why hadn't being a teacher worked out for me? Wasn't that my life purpose?

Many years later when I was trying to figure out what to do with the next phase of my life, I again was drawn to the idea of teaching. This time, I reviewed the idea not only with my mind, but with all my senses. I looked into teaching in the local school system. It made sense: easy commute, great hours, summers off. Yet there was a nagging feeling that this path was not quite right. And when I envisioned myself in an elementary school classroom, I felt a knot starting in my stomach. So, I passed on the local opportunity and kept looking. I asked myself what it was about teaching that I loved. I realized that communicating messages of significance, bringing new awarenesses to my students, and helping others on their journeys were the things I really loved about being a teacher. When I was able to look at teaching from that new, wider perspective, I then was able to find a career that utilized those key skills – and here I am today.

Sandra Ingerman, a licensed marriage and family therapist and professional mental health counselor, describes a similar experience in her book, *Shamanic Journeying*. She recounts receiving the thought that she should garden more. She tried to incorporate gardening into her schedule, but the combination of travel and living in an area that was not very fertile brought frustration. Finally, one day, it dawned on her that gardening was a metaphor for her life. What she realized she needed to do was to plant more seeds of love, hope and inspiration through her teaching, and work with clients to help them grow. Her ability to view life not literally, but as a metaphor, has helped both her clients and her to expand and grow.

The term "balance" is one that too often also gets taken literally. In the corporate world, the term "work/life balance" is bantered about as if there is a formula of just the right amount of work vs. home life that will produce feelings of contentment and well-being. The reality is that balance implies and requires acceptance. How often have I said that I was "out of balance" when really I was unhappy or dissatisfied with my life? In order to have balance, there have to be opposing forces in play. The art of finding balance is in acknowledging these forces, allowing them to coexist, and maintaining an awareness and acceptance of them in your life.

A client recently said to me, "So, even if I feel I am out of balance, I really could be in balance, right?" Taken literally, I believe I would have to refer that person out for other professional help! However, now that I was on the path to learning how to look at life differently, I had to smile and agree. Life is much more than our need to be continually happy, and balance is not a state of control. It is when you are able to see the yin and the yang, the positive and negative forces in your life, and begin to embrace them all that you are able to find that contentment with life and that metaphor called balance.

Turning 85

I TURNED 85 LAST week.

I can see it now: Those of you who don't know me are thinking, "Hmmm, I didn't think she was that old." Those who don't know me but saw my picture may have thought, "She looks pretty good for 85," or "That must be an old picture." And those who do know me are either thinking "That's a typo," or "Darn, I missed her birthday again."

But really, a few weeks ago, on some level I felt as if I had turned about 85. I almost hesitate to use that number though, as my Dad turned 85 recently and I realized that I was behaving even older than he was. What happened was this: I have been struggling with migraines for the past few years and saw a new doctor who put me on new medication. Always eager to please those in authority, I jumped at something that may prevent my being awakened at 2 a.m. with a throbbing temple and a desire to excavate my eyeball. Besides she told me that this medication causes weight loss. Magic words!

Week one on this transformative drug was like slogging through oatmeal. Everything was fuzzy, I felt doped up, I forgot words, and I still got headaches. I did lose five pounds, which in a very sick way made it seem almost worthwhile. I called the doctor and she assured me it was okay and just hang in there. And after about 5 days the fuzziness lifted and so did the headaches. I was lulled into a false sense of hope. By the start of week 2, however, I was noticing that I was just not myself and was working extremely hard to maintain appearances that I was the same old me. I just wasn't. I went online and found a site where you could put in your symptoms. Seemed I was either chemically poisoned or pregnant. Interesting.

The first thing that was gone was my energy. I had none. And it wasn't that I was physically tired – it was a soul energy. I had no energy for life. My brain was not firing on all cylinders. It was rare that I could complete three full sentences in a row without searching for a word or two. I easily became disoriented: missed my exit twice trying to get home. Details were easily overlooked: I showed up for a networking event on time – but a week early. It seems that I missed seeing the date on the flyer. All these things are really not good when you are starting a new job and are trying to prove yourself to your boss during the company's busiest time of the year! Between the stress of the job, the embarrassment of my deteriorating intelligence and the lack of interest in life in general, I found myself slipping into a depression. I became a magnet for negativity at a time when the news was oozing with it. And finally, I was hit hard by word of my friend Carol's death, and was teased by a jealous thought that floated around my head: why did she get to escape all of this when I didn't. It was that thought, along with my depression, and the constant and increasingly insistent pleading from my fiancé to call my doctor and get off this medication, that finally jolted me into action. I made the call and am now weaned off the headache drug. And I am happy – no ecstatic – to say that I am feeling alive again!

What I learned from this experience is three-fold:

1) I learned what it is like to feel old and devoid of energy. I really felt like I had aged significantly overnight and the disorientation and embarrassment at not being able to find common words during conversation made me want to isolate myself even further. I understand that feeling now. I get it now that when people say, "Look on the bright side!" that sometimes you hear the words and they make sense, but the connection between the intellect and the skill to tap into the feeling is missing. I had lost my ability to "will" myself happy.

I didn't have the life energy to do it. But what kept me going were two things I did still have: obligations – a family to care for, a job to do – and people who didn't give up on me. Therefore, I clearly see the importance of having something meaningful in your life for which you are responsible: a family member, a pet, a social obligation, a job or volunteer position. And I also see the importance of letting those in your family who are elderly know that they still are cared for and thought about, even if you can't be there with them all the time.

2) I learned firsthand the dangers of over-medication. Whether mine was a reaction to the drug I took or a drug combination, it doesn't really matter. Bottom line, it wasn't working and it was making me worse. What is important is that if you have a family member who is exhibiting any of the signs that I mentioned – disorientation, depression, changes in personality, lack of energy – get them to their doctor and get them checked out. By myself, I would not have done it. I would have kept going on the medication until my next appointment, partially because that is my personality and partially because I was so zonked out that I didn't really know any better. Over-medication is a serious problem and you can be a huge ally in helping your loved ones get the help they need before it gets to be a serious problem.

3) If you have practiced self-care in the past, your skills will kick in automatically. When I was both ultimately stressed (with blood pressure at 159/95) and disoriented and staring at a massive "To Do" list, I instinctively knew that the first thing I needed to do was to meditate. A 10-minute meditation calmed both my body and mind and made it easier to cope and think. Had I not been practicing self-care in the past, I probably would have kept charging ahead, writing this now from a hospital bed instead of at home while sipping tea and listening to Mozart.

Life is good again. Thank goodness!

Redefining Holidays

MY PARENTS ARE MIDWESTERN Conservative Hippies. Or at least that is the label that best matches how I see them. Well, actually I think it's just my Mom, but my Dad is a good-natured guy who'll do whatever she's doing, so he fits my description by default. I've been trying to find a way to explain the reason why they are the way they are. This description seems to be the best, all encompassing one that I've come up with so far.

For as long as I can remember, my mother has marched to her own drummer and eschewed the establishment. She has been growing her own vegetables since I was a child, writing letters of protest against perceived injustices and she gave up on organized religion years ago. She's driven me crazy with her recycling of everything from plastic bags to wrapping paper to teabags. Of course she composts. They've never owned a microwave (why bother?), don't own a computer and still have a rotary phone in the basement. No need to throw out those things that still work.

Lest you think I grew up in some commune, let's just say it's an area of the country that might be home to more than a couple of flag-waving, teabag-toting, *real* Americans. The kind that eat casseroles and Miracle Whip and JELL-O salads and wash them down with lots of pop.

So when my Mom announced to me that they were going to celebrate Thanksgiving this year on Monday instead of Thursday, due to schedules and weather possibilities, I thought...oh, why not? Normal families would shudder in horror at the thought of not celebrating the national holiday actually ON the national holiday but not a Midwestern Conservative Hippie family, right? In my mind, I needed this label in order for Monday to make sense....

I had my own Thanksgiving with my family at my home and moved quickly on to the next holiday preparations. All through the lists of things to do and buy and make and put up and address and, and, and…..I was just NOT feeling it! Try as I might, this holiday season was a struggle for me. And then I had one of those "out of body" experiences on Christmas Eve as I was rushing around trying to finish my shopping: A Japanese store clerk thanked me for my purchase and wished me a happy holiday. I wasn't quite sure what to say to her in response. As I left the store with my multiple bags and her voice in my head, I noticed the other harried shoppers with their multiple bags and wondered what someone from another country must think of us crazed Americans, overspending for this one over-commercialized day.

Today, two days after Christmas, I awoke very happy. I couldn't put my finger on it but there was something definitely different. It wasn't just a couple of good night's sleep. As I stood and stared at the beautiful snow that had blanketed us overnight I realized what it was: I had finally gotten my Christmas spirit! There were no lists I had to consult, no time sensitive activity that needed to be done. All I needed to do in that moment – post holiday, post stress – was to feel the joy of the season – Finally!

So maybe next year I'll do things differently. Maybe we'll do fewer gifts, and have more quality time together. Maybe I'll forgo the cards and give up the fights over hanging the lights outside. Maybe we'll even open our presents a day or two later and avoid the crowds and shopping rush!

Which makes me think….maybe my Mom is on to something after all….

Making Every Day Mother's Day

I HAD THE BEST Mother's Day this year! The enjoyment started the night before when my daughter looked at me seriously and said, "You are sleeping in tomorrow!" Music to my ears! That in itself would have been present enough for me. But the next day I was awakened to a chorus of "Happy Mother's Day!" as the requisite breakfast in bed was delivered, and then they left me alone to watch my favorite Sunday morning TV show in peace. I couldn't stop smiling.

The rest of the day was lovely too. I worked out, went for a walk, planted flowers and was treated to a gourmet dinner prepared again by the kids. I went to bed that night with the same smile I'd worn all day.

I'd like every day to be Mother's Day, please.

I was thinking about what made it so wonderful. First of all there were the loving intentions. Everything that was done was done consciously out of love. Next was the fact that I was doing what I enjoyed. I didn't once feel that I "had" to do anything – I did what I did because it was what I wanted to do. And believe me, working out is not always high on the "Want To Do" list! But my attitude that day made the exercise seem great: The feeling of having an onerous task to complete was replaced with gratitude for the time and ability to do something good for myself.

And finally, I was totally "in the day." I was not worried about tomorrow or yesterday. I wasn't stressing over what should be done. I was in the moment and relishing each activity.

So maybe I can't have Mother's Day itself more than once a year, but I sure can recreate the positive intentions, the doing what I want, and the living in the moment. Sounds like a recipe for happiness to me! And I won't even need a Hallmark card.

Chapter Two
Holding Back And Letting Go

Letting Go

When I was a freshman in college, the cheery, lemon-cream-colored cement block walls of my dorm room were covered with posters resplendent with inspirational sayings. My favorite was the one with the butterfly motif that said, "If you love something, let it go. If it comes back, it was meant to be." It had that touch of heartbreak and melodrama with a smidgen of optimism that resonated with my 18-year-old view of life. Ah, to be a martyr for love – a truly noble calling!

While I did become the Joan of Arc of the lovelorn for a time, "letting go" with practiced, painful panache, I didn't seem to ever achieve the second part of the saying – the coming back part. In my mind, the coming back was a guy realizing that he had made the biggest mistake of his life, returning to me with flowers, and begging for forgiveness, at which point I immediately would declare that all was forgiven and we would ride off into the sunset together. Surprisingly, that scenario just never happened. I came to write off that adage as a pithy attempt at, well, selling posters to 18-year-old girls. But what I never understood, was that it wasn't about an eternal hope for the prize – it was about letting go of the attachment to that prize. Now, years later, I'm beginning to get the message.

There have been many things in the last few years that I've had to learn to release: some literally, some emotionally, some mentally. In a lot of cases, I harbored a secret wish that those things would come back to me. But the amazing truth is that when I release not only a situation, but more importantly, my attachment to the outcome, things have a way of working out. How many times have I plotted and planned how something should work out, only to be disappointed? And conversely, how many times have I had an incredible time when I was able to "go with the flow"? It is not that I should give up the "prep work" – it's the expectation of the result that needs the release.

In starting my business there was a lot of prep work that needed to be done. I'd never done anything like that before. I had a vision, but not necessarily an expectation, of how it would all come together. I truly was in the flow of things and I was swept along in an amazing fashion with doors opening left and right. It was such an example to me of doing the next right thing, letting go, and seeing what was placed in my path. I was living and loving the process, without the preconceived notion of how it should or would be.

So you'd think I learned my lesson.

The next time I faced a challenge, instead of using my new-found insight and doing what I had JUST done – taking the next step and trusting the process – I somehow decided I now KNEW how things were supposed to work. I think by now you know how that assumption turned out.

So after realizing once again, that perhaps my way doesn't work, I've come up with a new mantra: "How can I serve?" At least for today I've realized that what I do is not all about me. I have come to believe that life affords you ALL sorts of opportunities to try out your new skills. I am the messenger, the conduit, the enabler of something beyond me. I have unique skills and talents that allow me to bring things to fruition, for which I am grateful. I've come to realize that serving means utilizing whatever skills I have, regardless of any judgment I may have put on them in the past. I used to think that serving meant a huge commitment, but now see it could be as simple as making a sales clerk smile. I just never know how something I do, no matter how insignificant it may seem to me, could affect someone else's life.

I'm still an optimist and still the person who wants to makes things happen. Those traits are part of my gifts. Martyrdom? Been there, done that. Today, that saying on my college poster speaks to me not of martyrdom, but of freedom. I'm letting go of rigid expectations that took up so much energy and space in my life in the past. And who knows what I just might get in return. I'm looking forward to it... without expectation!

Just Do It!

MY OLDEST SON IS passionate about skiing. He's also obsessed with snow. Ever since he first was buckled into skis when he was 4-years-old, he continues to be at his happiest when zooming down the slopes, over and over again. I'll forever remember the image of my otherwise seriously intense child, smiling and humming aloud as he streaked down the hill past me.

My son chose to attend his last two years of high school at a ski academy where he literally *lived* skiing, living alongside others who found his constant monitoring of the snowfall amounts a normal thing. How wonderful to be able to fully live the life you love!

I've learned an awful lot from this son during our years together so far, not the least of which is to recognize and embrace my own passions. When I think back to when I was his age, I have a hard time thinking of anything I was that passionate about, except maybe boys. It wasn't so much that I didn't have any interests, as much as that I didn't allow myself to become too passionate about them. Moderation was my watchword. More important, if I poured my soul into something, and then didn't "do well" or wasn't accepted by others as a result, it would be too much for me to take. People asked me if my son was training for the Olympics, and the answer was, "No." He skis because he loves it. Bottom line, end of story.

Following your bliss is something, so often, foreign to so many of us. Just the thought of it elicits sighs and comments such as, "Wow, wouldn't that be nice?" Yes, wouldn't it?! Then why don't we do it? Is it because we are too busy, too afraid, too poor, too over-committed or just too tired? Maybe what others would think – or what you suppose they would think – stops you in your tracks. Whatever the reasons, you're denying yourself and the world the benefit of your highly-charged positive energy. And we all could use some more of that these days!

What happens when someone follows their bliss? I'm not talking about dropping everything, quitting your job and moving to Alaska kinds of things. I'm talking about recognizing that there is something you really love to do and then making the time to do it. What happens when you make the effort is analogous to lighting charcoal soaked in lighter fluid versus trying to light charcoal that has not been soaked. The soaked briquettes effortlessly exude energy, making the barbeque experience that much more enjoyable. Likewise, when someone commits to doing something that they enjoy, their natural spark ignites an internal energy source and sends it out in the universe for all of us to enjoy and utilize.

If you could do anything you wanted to do, if there were no time constraints or money constraints or social constraints of any kind, what would you do? Would you take that dance class? Go roller blading or snowboarding? Would you spend 15 minutes a day escaping into a romance novel? Whatever your bliss might be, discover it, embrace it and DO IT! Life is too short and the world too full of negativity to let your opportunities pass you by.

And if your bliss should take you skiing out west, and you're passed by a smiling downhill racer, tell him his mom says hello!

Making a Personal Course Correction

DURING A RECENT HOLIDAY season, I felt that everyone around me was stupid. Like there was a conspiracy somewhere and I was the lucky one who got tested on just how much stupidity I could handle. I was losing that battle. It was the moment when I felt that my children also had lost all their intelligence, that I decided that perhaps the issue just MIGHT be with someone other than everyone else in the world. I hate it when it all comes back to me.

I can, for the most part, handle pretty large amounts of stress. I've worked hard at creating a balance in my life so that stress doesn't create a problem for me or those around me. But this time the balance got away from me. The signs were probably there, but I was in a Scarlett O'Hara groove ("I'll think about it tomarrah…") and didn't acknowledge it. Sometimes I know the signs are there but I just can't see them – a little like my son's car dashboard which flashes an ominous "CHECK INFO DISPLAY" message, but the LCD on that display is broken. Well, it's trying to tell us something, but who knows what it is – so we just ignore it and keep going. Or sometimes the signs are very obvious and I still ignore them. Like my "Low Fuel" light glaring at me. Funny, those things really are telling the truth, as I recently discovered when I had to be pushed across an intersection when I stalled out. I had been on my way to the gas station, but had to make just a couple more stops first….

But aside from the literal signs, there are other things that can or should catch my attention: desires to isolate, thought patterns that are negative, and of course, the conviction that I am surrounded by imbeciles. It brought to mind the work of Dr. Masaru Emoto and his work with water crystals. Dr. Emoto, in his book *The Messages of Water*, studied the effect of words, thoughts and prayer on water. He would place water in a container and tape a typewritten word or phrase on it and let it sit overnight. He then would freeze the water and photograph their crystals. The power of the words is amazing to behold. The water with positive words produced beautiful crystals and the water with negative ones produced misshapen crystals. It reminds me that when I think negative thoughts, use negative words, or expect negative actions, that is what I will get.

The next time I start believing that the world has lost its marbles, I am going to stop, breathe, and make a course correction. Life lived in resentment is wasted time. My desire is to live a life of abundance: abundant happiness, abundant health, abundant prosperity, abundant love. I am now in complete gratitude for all the lessons and blessings that have resulted from those gifts and look forward to reaping more rewards in the future. I wish you all the same and more.

The Fall of Denial

I DIDN'T WANT TO admit it. I kept myself very busy, always looking down. I avoided any discussion on the topic. And then I turned the corner today and caught a splash of vibrant orange and golden yellow magnified by the indescribable vibrant, blue sky and it took my breath away, along with all my defenses. I had to admit it – I really love fall.

I've been avoiding admitting that to myself this year, as I kept thinking back to last year's seemingly endless blandness once the precious leaves had left the trees. I didn't want to enjoy the juiciness of this magnificent season because it makes me admit that yes, this too shall pass. As if I held my breath long enough, denied the crunching of leaves underfoot, and kept my nose to the grindstone, it would put off the inevitable. Another reminder to me of how strong (and at times ridiculous) the human psyche can be.

If I can deny myself the pleasure of the autumnal moment, what else am I capable of denying myself? How many "precious moments" have I let slip by with my children because I was too busy? How many times did I avoid an interaction with them because underneath is the reality of a deeply-buried fear of their growing up: if I don't admit it, it isn't so. Stated so plainly it sounds, indeed, a bit insane. Actually, the insanity is in realizing it and still proceeding in the same way.

I've been fortunate, of late, to have been given opportunities to put these new-found awarenesses into practice. Today's visual feast was one such moment. I've also developed relationships, both personally and professionally, which test my resolve for control. Is it possible to let go, to trust others, to possibly even (gasp!) *enjoy* not being the one in control? Well, I'm still working on that one!

Denial is a supremely human reaction which, in its best case, protects us from the hurt and danger we are not able to face. It's like hitting the mute button so we don't have to hear it. And control is the mechanism to keep denial in its place. I remember hitting the mute button while watching television when my children were little when I anticipated a not-so-child-friendly phrase about to be uttered. This small flash of repression was acceptable until they were old enough to understand. Continuing the denial and control past that point, out of habit or fear, does nothing more than prolong the inevitable and stymies growth along the way. Learning to face realities, and learning to let go, while momentarily painful, always creates more freedom in the long run.

My denial of the beauty of the season, and attempt to deny the impending winter months fortunately were short-lived. Whether I was caught off guard, or was ready to accept the realities, I can't be sure. What I can say for certain is that even for that brief moment, when I was smacked by the beauty of the fall scenery and brought squarely into the here and now, I felt supremely happy and at peace. Maybe if I can enjoy each luscious autumn day while they are here, the winter won't be so bad.

And if not, at least I can't deny that spring will come again.

Responsible Adventure

AT THE LAST MINUTE, my eldest son scored tickets to the Rose Bowl game and within 48-hours was texting me "Greetings from 73-degree California." The boy knows how to push buttons... He had no idea what he was doing for New Year's Eve, no clue where he was staying, and no real plan for how to get back to school in Oregon. I wavered between parental horror and absolute admiration – and jealousy – at his ability to go with the flow and make things happen.

As my other children and I sat around the dinner table shaking our heads at their older brother's adventures, I realized that, although at first glance you'd never know it, I am really a lot like him, only with a few more layers of responsibility. This awareness came to me as I recounted the story of how I moved to Boston. I had gotten a new job with IBM and was transferring away from my cow neighbors (literally) in Vermont to a hopefully, livelier lifestyle, befitting a single person in her 20s. The only person I knew in Boston was an ex-boyfriend to whom I was not speaking. I knew nothing about the town and had no idea where I was going to live. All I had planned was that on Monday I was packing my car and driving to Boston. On the Saturday before I left, I decided to go skiing one more time, by myself, and while on a chairlift, met a guy from Marblehead, a town north of Boston. He introduced me to his parents, who immediately invited me to stay with them and help me find a place to live. I did, and within a day, found a great apartment and a roommate with whom I keep in touch to this day. I don't remember ever worrying about the move or any of the details, in the same way that my son did not worry about his trip to California. I possessed a calm faith that the details would work out – and by golly, they did.

I need to remember this story because it shows me that 1) the answers appear when you have faith and ALLOW them to emerge, and 2) I've done it before and I can do it again. My challenge is to learn to view the parameters of my life not as restrictive, but as reflections of the choices I've made. Responsibility is a ballast that gives my life direction and focus, and keeps me from floating, adrift, in a sea of possibilities.

I'd love to just take off on an adventure like my son, but age does bring a certain amount of wisdom, and ignoring reality has its own share of issues. Perhaps, instead, I can choose to view my present life as my adventure and be open to new possibilities. Hey, you never know...

Physics 101

THERE WERE CERTAIN COURSES in high school that I never thought would have any practical application in my life. Trigonometry was one of them. Try as hard as he might, Mr. Steinbeck could NOT convince me that not only was Trig a worthwhile use of my time, but that the offer to enroll in HONORS Trig was nothing short of a privilege afforded to only a chosen few. To this day I still feel a little smug when I think about how I, for one of the first times in my life, stuck to my position and wasn't wooed by the pretense of fame and fortune being dangled in front of me in the form of a math teacher's dream.

Physics was another one. I just never thought I'd need to know the how and why about the way things work. "They happen" worked for me. Obviously I had not yet ever been faced with moving my household.

A few years ago, when I was full of life and optimism and energy, I was finishing up my master's degree, finalizing a divorce, and starting a new business. I mentioned to a colleague that I was thinking of maybe selling my house too. In a very calm voice – probably to hide the terror that she wanted to scream out to me – she proclaimed, "Moving takes a lot of energy." I believe that this was the first physics lesson that really made sense to me.

I am winding up a three-week, non-stop moving extravaganza this week when I turn over the keys to my big seven-bedroom home and can focus solely on finding room for the overwhelming amount of STUFF in my new three-bedroom Cape. "Moving takes a lot of energy" is, I have found, an understatement! On all levels – physical, emotional, mental – it is draining. It's also a good way to lose weight, although I won't be trying it again anytime soon!!

Through all of the angst and exhaustion, I also have had time to learn a bit more about physics and other subjects that I never thought would be applicable to my life. Things about volume and leverage and how moving company employees are masters at both. I've learned about angles and mass and the proper way to tilt mattresses to wind them around charming, but impractical, staircases. I've learned how to apply enough force and use the banister as a lever when trying to lift a box spring up and into the house via a second floor patio door. I've learned about the force that is applied when one's moving partner doesn't know your hands have slipped off the dresser and its entire weight lands on your leg.

But the greatest lesson I have learned is this: matter expands to fit the space. Somehow, over the course of 16 years, we had managed to completely fill a very large house with a lot of not-so-much-needed stuff, a fact about which I believe my mother is secretly saying, "I told you so." If you have the space, it will be filled. It seems Zen qualities, not to mention physics, were not prevalent in my life.

There is one area in which this principle took on a very special and profound meaning. I learned that if I created a space for people to help me, they did. They filled up the void that I had created with humor and warmth and generosity of spirit. It was a matter of my learning to open up and allow the rest to flow. And Mary, Fran, Deborah and Regina all came rushing in to give selflessly – a lesson that has had more of an impact on me that any honors class ever did. I am amazed and truly grateful!!

Perhaps by the time I write again I'll even have a better idea where my pencil sharpener may be or where that special place was that I put my extra credit cards so I wouldn't lose them. I do know now that if I continue to apply those physics principles, and create space for more love and goodness to flow on in, it will. I'm grateful to be able to learn my physics lessons now, even if I couldn't see their purpose back in high school.

Honors Trig? Still not seeing it....

Janet M. Neal

Becoming Visible

AT CHURCH ON SUNDAY I was asked to participate in several parts of an upcoming service, including writing and reading my own prayers. Just call me "Pastorette Neal." I actually had done it once before and didn't remember any lasting trauma from it. However, I successfully had managed to avoid being called upon for the past 12 years to do this duty again: the equivalent of avoiding eye contact and staying under the radar the entire time that your kids are in school. This was not an easy task for someone who loves the spotlight, mind you. It illustrates the skill I have learned very effectively: how to make myself invisible in close quarters. It must have been that Facebook birthday greeting I sent to the person who does the Sunday scheduling that brought me back into the church's consciousness. That'll teach me!

This was not going to be a difficult task for me, or so it seemed on paper. Besides, if I could sing in Latin with the choir in front of the congregation, reading words I had written myself should be a walk in the park.

Writing the prayers, however, was more difficult than I thought. For one, I was trying to think of how they usually sound and realized that I either have a very limited memory, or I am not paying attention during the services. I believed that, although those possibilities were both true, the latter was really the issue. The only thing that comforted me was that if I weren't really paying attention, probably others weren't either, and they probably wouldn't start listening just because I was the one at the lectern.

The second issue is that my views have, shall we say, strayed from traditional Presbyterianism. Over the years I have spent time in California (enough said) and obtained a master's in spiritual psychology. My beliefs are founded on my traditional church upbringing, liberally sprinkled with beliefs pulled from a variety of global spiritual sources. I didn't think that my staid, Presbyterian congregants would react quite so positively to my message if I kept saying I was "sending them Light and Love." So the challenge became how to express myself within the comfortable confines of the institution that asked me to do this service.

Lastly, there was that issue of logistics. I couldn't even remember when we were to stand or sit, or which chair I was supposed to use (there were two chairs up front - did it matter which one I sat in?). And what if I forgot my reading glasses?! Fortunately, I typed my readings in large enough font to avoid that issue, and the minister graciously let me know when to do the rest. The only thing I forgot was to ask the congregation to stand before I launched into my first responsive reading, leaving many looking bewildered and very few actually chiming in with the group response. There were one or two words stumbled over and then I finally got my sea legs and it was smooth sailing from there on out.

At the end of the service, when I was in the "receiving line" greeting the congregation on their exit from the sanctuary, people said "Nice job," and I responded with "Well, except for that beginning..." After hearing myself say it enough times, it finally hit me how I was discounting myself. A simple smile and a "Thank You!" would have been the appropriate responses. Why is that I feel the need to put myself down instead of stepping into my greatness? Why am I so uncomfortable with being acknowledged for doing a good job – is it feeling that I am making someone else feel bad in the process, or do I feel that I am undeserving of the praise? I know I still harbor some very old belief that it is wrong to think highly of yourself – a belief that just may have its origins in the very institution I was now representing. Perhaps this exercise was a way for me to learn to let that misguided lesson go.

I don't think I'll be running out and signing up for seminary anytime soon, but I am sure I'll be doing a presentation of some kind in the near future. I'm going to make sure that I acknowledge the good work I have done, letting go of anything that doesn't meet my unrealistic view of perfection. And if anyone happens to give me a compliment, I'll remember to answer with a simple, "Thanks!" And maybe I'll throw in a little "light and love to you," just for good measure!

I Dreamed a Dream...

I DREAMT THAT I was at a business conference in Utah and during a break I decided to buy a dog – a very large, white, furry dog, like a Great Pyrenees. It was the greatest thing – until I realized that I had no idea how to get it home. I panicked, focusing on how I didn't have enough money to transport the dog and berating myself for not thinking this through. All I can say is that I am glad that my purchase was a dream!

The interesting thing about dreams is how they play out unconscious thoughts and beliefs. To me, a dog is something I love. If I followed through on the dream's action, I was in a position where I was fearful of losing what I loved because I didn't have what it took to keep it. And because I was focused totally on the lack of funds, I could not come up with creative solutions. It was a dream, for goodness sake: I could have had a kind stranger come and give me the money I needed – or buy me an airplane – or move my home to Utah – or have the dog and I sprout wings and fly home! But, obviously, my issue du jour was to examine my focus on "the lack of" something that I needed.

It is so important to realize the attitude from which you operate. Is your attitude coming from a position of lack or poverty consciousness, or one of abundance? Do you worry that someone else will take your slice of the pie, or do you believe that the pie will just be made larger as needed? Life has a way of accommodating your mindset.

In looking further at my dream, I was forced to look at other parts of my life. Where else was I approaching things from a feeling of lack? Well, take eating. I am eating like there is no tomorrow these days! I believe that there is no cookie safe from my grasp within a two-mile radius. The holidays and the associated gift-buying certainly start doing a number on my mind and wallet, causing me to think the well is running dry. And I even can draw the analogy to relationships, where I can find myself fearing the worst for no apparent reason. The fear associated with lack can be very persistent and very pervasive.

This holiday season is a wonderful time to remind myself of the gift of abundance. To shift from a mindset of lack, to this wondrous attitude, truly opens up possibilities. Regardless of one's faith, holiday stories are resplendent in their messages of hope and optimism and abundance. This attitude is mine to embrace, if I choose to do so.

Tonight, maybe I'll dream about snuggling up with my gorgeous husband and that furry love bundle in my new home overlooking the ocean – the one I bought after I wrote that motivational best-seller that Oprah just LOVED. Hey, if you're going to embrace abundance, you might as well think big!

Puppy Love

Six weeks before my puppy and I began to attend Puppy Kindergarten, I thought that I had the cutest, smartest, most perfect pet. Once our classes began, however, I learned what my pup, Lily, really was supposed to be like – and my opinion of her changed drastically! Gone was the amazing creature I had brought to the training center. In her place was a nervous, unsocial animal who, if I didn't act quickly, might develop some fairly obnoxious and potentially dangerous habits. I guess my pre-class ignorance truly was bliss!

Ever since my consciousness-raising classes in high school where we rigorously worked to debunk labels ascribed to toys that supposedly were appropriate for girls or for boys, I have been acutely aware of the dangers of making blanket statements about a person, place or thing. I prided myself on the fact that when I was a teacher, I refused to read my students' "permanent records" prior to getting to know them, lest I might be influenced by what others thought. And I worked diligently to avoid using any kind of pigeon-holing terms when referring to my students, lest I stifle their individuality.

Yeah, yeah, yeah. I am here to say now that my best intentions, while honorable, only served to mask the truth. I am a human being. I am subject to the same desires and influences as the next person. And if there is someone whom I think knows more than I do, well, then, I guess they must be right and I'll accept their labels for me, too. So, it seemed that my darling little pup was a potential threat if I didn't deal with her behavior now.

As usual, I dove into the responsibility. We practiced our "sits" and "downs." We visited places with unfamiliar people and animals to make her more comfortable around strangers. We walked, and stopped when she tugged, taking an inordinate amount of time to circumvent the block. And she did very, very well. (OK, with appropriate apologies to the high school baseball team: I forgot that she has this ball fetish....)

I returned to Puppy Kindergarten the next week beaming with pride, all set to accept praise modestly, and ready to show them a thing or two. And she was great! I was again, the very proud "parent."

There is a saying that "expectations are premeditated resentments."...

The following week I returned to class expecting Lily to be the star student again. Perhaps it was the alignment of the planets, or that she'd had a bad dream and hadn't slept well, or maybe she was just reflecting her master's momentary unfocused nature, but she was terrible. I was NOT happy. I had such expectations of her being a certain way and BAM! She certainly gave me reason to be angry with her. That unconditional love nonsense flew right out the window.

Which makes me reflect on the rest of my life....

If I look back at the times in my life when I was the most upset, I probably can find the expectation I held that created the unhappiness. If I could replay those scenarios again, without the expectations, most of the "justified" indignation would vanish.

I find that relationships of any kind are ripe with expectations. There are roles we are expected to play, goals we are expected to meet and things we are expected to do. I can think back to when my kids were babies and I just loved them – nothing more, nothing less – both because I didn't have any experience as a parent, but also because I didn't have any expectations for their behavior. But when they hit a certain age, I became guilty of expecting things that could not help but cause angst, if not anger, something a few blocks south of unconditional love.

I find it the same in a romantic relationship: in the beginning there are no expectations. There is joy in the getting to know and celebration of who the other person is. Each nuance is a wonderful surprise unfurled and love abounds in the discovery. My challenge is in learning how to cross over into that next phase without setting up hurdles of unexpressed expectations for my partner to jump over along the way.

As I look at my still-adorable pup snoozing on the hearth in front of me, I am grateful and amazed at all this little (and growing like a weed!) creature has taught me in a few short months. I somehow don't think that she is chatting with the other dogs in the neighborhood and comparing notes on how great or lousy a master I am. And if she is, those "I can't love you enough!" kisses when she greets me each morning are even a more poignant example of what unconditional love is all about. I "expect" that she'll be teaching me even more life lessons as our journey together continues.

Escaping (My Mind's) Reality

I'VE ALWAYS BEEN A vacation kind of gal. You know those people who, at the end of the year, still have unused vacation days? That has NEVER been me! One of my favorite things about the beginning of a new year is being able to plan out my time off. This preference is, however, not something I recommend bringing up in a job interview!

A conversation I recently had with a friend reminded me of my first experience of vacationing with small children. I remember the usual excitement of planning the trip, the thought of getting away from the normal routine, and the anticipation of relaxing with a good book by the pool, with the occasional nap thrown in for good measure. Those of you who are parents can stop laughing now. What I discovered is that the word "vacation" is a misnomer for those who are traveling with little ones: the word really means "life in a new location." And with the disruption in routine, it actually can be more stressful than just staying at home!

Vacation to me has always been synonymous with "escape." That is why the book *Eat, Pray, Love* by Elizabeth Gilbert has been so wildly successful: it chronicles one woman's year-long escape from reality as she takes a series of amazingly adventuresome vacations around the world. Even some women I know, who are happy in their careers and at home, harbor a secret desire to be able to leave it all behind, if just for a little while.

I loved the book and yes, would love to experience what the main character did. A few years back I would have given, well, perhaps my first born child for that chance! But from where I sit today, the desire to escape is, thankfully, not paramount in my thinking. *Freedom* is really what I desire and freedom, I have learned, has both external and internal components. In our country we are free to do, say, or go where we want, within reason. And yet there remains a desire by many to escape. What those people are focusing on are the external constraints of their lives and wishing to be rid of their bondage.

Real freedom, however, comes not from external release but from an internal sense of serenity. It's the knowing that, regardless of everything happening on the outside, inside all is well. Real freedom is a state of being that people expend a great deal of time, energy and resources trying to achieve, and yet that state of being really takes none of those efforts. Real freedom is learning to escape not from your physical reality, but from the expectations and machinations of your overactive mind. It is not escape from the bondage of a job, a relationship, a routine or an environment that brings freedom: it is the escape from the bondage of self.

I'm still looking forward to next year's vacation and I relish any breaks from my routine which give me a chance to relax and breathe. But gone is that urgency and desperate feeling of NEEDING to get away. Now if I feel antsy or overwhelmed, I know I have a choice to continue to live with the meddlesome mind that created my anxiety, or to take a mental vacation and choose a different scene on which to focus. Escaping the self-imposed limitations of my mind proves to be a satisfying, enjoyable and more economically advantageous trip – and I don't even have to ask for the day off!

Free to Be...

I HAD BREAKFAST THIS morning with a friend and our conversation brought me back to an awareness I experienced last week in my writing class. I was taking a favorite workshop – one I've taken for several years – and found myself intimidated by the other participants. They either were more experienced, more professional, more creative, younger or older than I. You name it, they were better. As a result, my writing was pretty *blah*. It totally reflected my view of myself. It was after two days of this self-imposed misery that I decided enough was enough. After all, why was I enrolled if not to be open to putting myself out there in order to learn and grow? And so I did – and my writing improved about 1000%. It was when I let go of the presumptions, and was unafraid to be real, that I found both freedom and the ability to connect with others.

This is what my friend was pointing out to me as she described a workshop she'd recently attended. She noted that one panelist seemed to take the "safer" route and, so, her comments were stilted. The other panelist had been willing to put it all out there, and my friend immediately felt a connection with her. So much so, that she went out and bought three of her books!

It's an interesting paradox: I hold back in order to be received better because I am afraid what others will think, and yet when I let go and release any worry about what someone else thinks, it brings others closer. Go figure!

Guess I need to keep working on it...

I Know It's Somewhere...

You should see my desk. Well, I think there is a desk underneath everything! The surface started off being organized. You almost can make out the neatly piled, collated-according-to-priority work, now overcome by bills and instruction manuals and fix-it guides. Best of intentions...

My "quick" weekend task was to upgrade my Blackberry to a newer model. This was after weeks of going back and forth on whether to go to the iPhone or stick with the tried and true. Knowing that I had enough chaos in my life, I went with the known entity. What should have been a simple process has now consumed my weekend and my desk. An upgrade to the software crashed my computer drive. Once I figured that out, I finally could install the balance of the software. I spent hours trying to figure out why I wasn't getting any mail before I finally got to the root of that problem. Last night I spent another three hours surfing the applications that could be downloaded. So much for "set it and forget it."

There is a saying "Your outer life reflects your inner world." Ugh. Truly I feel that my brain is a reflection of that desk. It is a series of things started and stopped when some other urgent need takes its place. And although the data may be there still, it is not easily retrievable. I know that there is something important in there that needs to be done, but heck if I can find it!

When my desk gets like this, I need to take the time to clean it off and reorganize it. It feels SO much better when I do. The same thing is true with my mind. I need to take the time to sit, to calm my thoughts, to allow the "stuff" in my head to settle back into their proper places so that I actually can retrieve it when I need it. I need to meditate and calm my body so that I am not a perpetual stress hormone factory. And I need to remember that the next time I see my desk, or my car, or my house starting to get this cluttered and unmanageable, it's a proverbial wake-up call to look inside again.

Off to do my cleaning...both inside and out. Never know what I'll find!

Stress is Our Friend

LIVING IN THE NEW York area, I was relieved to read recently that stress is necessary for growth. Nice to know that my surroundings are providing me with ample opportunity to enhance my life! I must admit a bit of skepticism, as well as relief, when contemplating that concept. After all, how can anything that can cause physical, emotional and mental problems be helpful?

The answer: moderation and balance.

In their book *The Power of Full Engagement*, Jim Loehr and Tony Schwartz explain how professional athletes use stress to improve their game. They explain that those athletes who push themselves beyond their comfort zones – and then rest and regroup – build muscle physically, mentally and emotionally. It's the same concept used in body building. As a muscle is pushed beyond its current capability (think Jane Fonda saying "Go for the burn!"), microscopic tears actually occur in it. When followed by a period of rest, the muscle rebuilds itself, filling in the broken parts with more mass and strength. The stress has actually helped build it stronger, but ONLY when followed by the time for reconstruction.

I seem to miss that second part of the process in my life. I am VERY good at the stressing part, but don't often remember the resting part. Actually, I don't think I value the resting part. I have been conditioned to think that recouping or resting is unproductive time, a waste of a valuable commodity. Rest is, in reality, what will give me the strength to tackle the ever-increasing challenges of my life.

Studies have proven that the body operates not only on circadian rhythms – that 24-hour cycle of sleep and activity – but also on ultradian rhythms. Ultradian rhythms are a shorter, more subtle cycles of energy use and regeneration occurring every 90-120 minutes. The body is actively engaged for that period of time, followed by a "down time" where it is looking for rest. Think about attending an event. About 90 minutes into it you start to yawn or fidget. It is a natural reaction to your body's need for rest and renewal. Standing up and stretching at intermission gives you just that, allowing you the ability to watch the second act. Or, at work, taking a five minute walk down the hall after a period of concentrated effort will re-energize you as well.

Some people have the luxury of taking a more extended rest period. During World War II, Winston Churchill took daily, 90-minute naps. He recognized that unless he rested, he would not be able to deal with the stress of his job.

Even if you can't afford such a large amount of time, a small break of five minutes will provide what the body requires. Five minutes of deep breathing, a ten minute cat nap, a few minutes of meditation, or a brisk walk around the block all serve the same function: allowing the body and mind to regroup and refresh. Rest gives you the strength to go back and face even a little more stress, as you now have worked to build your muscle in a healthy way.

So the next time I'm feeling stressed out, I'll take a breath and smile. I'm experiencing a growth opportunity! I'll grab for the gusto...... and won't forget the nap!

Chapter 3:
Good Enough

Grabbing the Rope

"Did you do it?" she bubbled.

"No, I grabbed the rope."

As I sat puzzling over that overheard exchange, I was grateful for the follow-up question:

"Is that good or bad?"

I was sitting at the café at the Omega Institute in Rhinebeck, NY, trying to write a piece for the next session of a workshop I was attending there. Around me were students who were taking classes in everything from yoga, to vortex healing, to visionary art, to trapeze flying. Yes, trapeze. There was a giant trapeze set up in the field next to my workshop classroom, open to anyone with the inclination to try it out. Apparently, my café mate had been one of those brave, or more foolish, souls. And evidently, when doing the trapeze, "grabbing the rope" is not a good thing. It is the equivalent of hitting the ejection button or screaming "uncle."

As she went on to describe her unsuccessful trip through the air, being caught by the instructor, and then not being able to turn back around to catch the swinging bar in time and being forced to "grab the rope", I found myself stuck on her first phrase: "As I was flying through the air..." How could she <u>possibly</u> say that her effort was a failure? Heck, if I even got up on the trapeze platform it would be a success! No, even before that – getting dressed in spandex and parading out in front of curious onlookers – now, <u>that</u> would be success!

While I sat silently chastising her for her apparent inability to see reality accurately, I became aware of a random, two-word thought starting to gather in my meddlesome mind. Like a gathering storm, I felt their ominous influence before they ever made their way directly into my consciousness. Their mantra was building steam.

Yeah, but…

I began to think of all the times that I had accomplished something – big or small – and ended a proud statement about my achievement with, "yeah, but _____" (fill in the blank with any self-deprecating phrase, such as, "It wasn't that hard," "I had a lot of help," "Anyone could do it," or "It's not important"). I am sure that to some, my equivalent of flying-through-the-air-only-to-grab-the-rope would be a major triumph, while I, like my overheard café compadre, would choose to focus only on the failure.

Yeah, but…

It's really only a matter of choice and the decision is up to us. We can welcome the "yeah, but" phrase as a reminder that look, "we're doing it again," and use that opportunity to reframe our perspective. We can choose to see the event as a process and celebrate our successes along the way. And we can choose to be grateful for that safety net that has allowed us to come back and try again another day.

That "yeah, but" mantra droned on in my head until even I got tired of it. Enough! With the lyrics of Helen Reddy's song echoing in my ears, I realized that "I am strong," and I am also curious and talented. I am grateful for each daily launch on this exciting trapeze swing of my life.

Even if, at times, I have to grab the rope.

Coming in the Front Door

MY JOURNEY INTO THE world of business was a rather circuitous adventure. While teaching elementary school I was offered a summer job as a security guard at a nearby GM plant by the father of one of my students. Never one to look a gift horse in the mouth, even if it meant looking like a female Barney Fife, I took the chance. This experience allowed me to get a job the following summer at IBM as, you guessed it, a security guard! Without going through my entire corporate career history, let's just say my jobs started there and advanced to others including receptionist, secretary, administrator, sales specialist and finally account manager. Whew – in only 19 years! So, when I look at my nephew who apparently waltzed out of college and into a cushy Wall Street job, I don't know whether to smile or cringe. Apparently he knew how to use the front door.

While growing up, I remember being told the adage, "Get your foot in the door." There was honor in starting out at the bottom and working your way up. I still believe that there is value in that process. The danger lies in thinking that you only are worthy of lower level positions and/or don't even try for anything more.

There is an analogy to that old adage about how to get ahead in the workplace. How do you best get a foot in the door…in life? I have found myself trying the backdoor approach, not only in the workplace, but in life situations. This is nothing new for me, as I can remember back as early as first grade asking little, redheaded Peter Maasen over to my house and playing a 45 record for him entitled "I Do", because I liked him and wanted to marry him. Needless to say, he didn't get the subtle message. I was much too afraid to just come out and say something about how I felt – God forbid he'd look at me the wrong way or (horrors) say I was stupid, or something worse! So, I preferred the "slip in the back door and right back out if necessary" approach.

I wonder how many opportunities I've missed because I let myself choose the backdoor. How many more people could I have met? How many new opportunities may I have had? How many relationships could have begun, or ended, sooner? There is no regret for my life as I have lived it, but, instead, a realization that I have gained the insight and so, now have the opportunity to choose the front door.

When I choose to approach life head on, I enter a new situation with an openness that cannot help but meet me halfway. If that new door closes, another opens. I don't have to spend time meandering down hallways of "what ifs" or "if onlys." I don't have to "settle" for something. I am self-honoring, self affirming, and self confident.

Walking in the front door requires focus. I must know where I want to go and do what it takes to get there. Going in the back entrance can get me there as well, but often, with that approach, I am forced to be led by others, rather than relying on myself to reach my goal. Coming in the front lets me clearly see where I am going and what I am headed into. Why come in through the alleyway when I can march boldly into the foyer? The front door is always available to me if I aim myself in its direction.

My path through the maze of my life has been filled with a lot of frustration, but also many successes and a lot of fun. Sometimes it takes time to figure out which door to approach. But, I'm grateful that I've now got my eyes on, and my hand reaching for, that shiny, brass knob and I'm ready to waltz on in. Open Sesame!

The Tablecloth

I HAD A VISION in a meditation today. I was presented with a tablecloth – a huge, white one, hand-spun from the softest of fibers. Its slightly yellow hue betrayed its age and, yet, gave it distinction and grace. It was entirely handcrafted and meticulously embroidered with a pattern of gorgeous intertwining flowers, decorated with seed pearls. I touched it and knew that the softness belied its strength. It was only after admiring it for a time, taking in its richness, did I notice two, tear-drop-shaped stains on one section, as if a coffee cup, removed in haste after a jubilant evening with friends, had left behind its own calling card. I noticed these stains, but didn't give them much thought, and moved back to take in the tablecloth's magnificence.

It was then that I stopped to wonder why I was being presented with this image. "What is this?" I asked.

"It is you," came the reply.

My eyes immediately focused back on the stains, noticing the imperfection in the piece. It was an old tablecloth, showing its age. Imperfection was evident to anyone who looked at it. I felt panic rising.

"It is you," came the reply again.

I looked again, this time from a higher perspective, and saw a magnificent, one-of-a-kind piece. Its flaws made it so. And so it is.

Dodging the Dream Squashers

Have you ever had the experience where you were really excited about something and couldn't wait to share it with your friend, your parents, or your spouse? You relish the opportunity to relive the thought or experience and then to have those whom you care about share in your joy and enthusiasm. You excitedly tell your story…and are met with a blank stare. Or a laugh. Or they aren't even listening.

I have.

My immediate reaction is emotional: disappointment, perhaps anger, feeling rejected, feeling foolish. But within those reactions are two truths: The first is that I had set up an expectation that had not been fulfilled. The second is that I'd just encountered a Dream Squasher.

Some believe that, "Those who abandon their dreams will discourage yours." And, as much as I don't want to admit it, I do have those types of people in my life. The key is to recognize who they are and not set myself up for disappointment. Expecting them to change when there is a pattern to their reactions of rejection is nothing short of insanity on my part.

Being an eternal optimist, I found this fact a very difficult pill to swallow. "Yeah, but what if THIS is the topic we'll bond on?" Yes, and if pigs could fly…. The truth is that it's just not a good idea to even go there. As Sonia Choquette says in her book, *Your Heart's Desire*, "Face it – people like to rain on the creative parade! Take a look at history. No one ever encouraged Leonardo da Vinci. Or the Wright brothers. Or Benjamin Franklin, Thomas Edison, Madame Curie…All were dismissed by the experts of their day as fools, dreamers, nuts, and quacks. The average naysayer hasn't changed much over the centuries. Pity them. Pray for them. Avoid them. But for Pete's sake, don't *consult* them when it comes to your dream! And ignore them when they offer unsolicited advice."

Just because someone doesn't gush over my dreams and experiences doesn't necessarily mean I cut them out of my life. They obviously are in my life for a reason, and they probably fulfill other needs of mine and are valuable to me. But it is worthwhile to become very aware of those who support me and those who don't.

When I have a dream that I want to pursue, a goal I want to achieve or an idea I want to explore, I need to have a trusted, supportive person or persons in my life on whom I can rely. I think of my dreams as my babies – I need to protect them and nurture them. I need support from those who will help me in my efforts. Sometimes, it is my family that fills that bill; at other times, it is a network of friends or professionals, such as coaches, therapists, or co-workers, who will be there for me and give me the help I need to see my dreams reach fruition.

Cherish your dreams, your ideas and your enthusiasm. Surround yourself with those who will help illuminate your path. Don't let a Dream Squasher deny the world of the beauty of your potential!

I Want MORE!

EVER SINCE I CAN remember, I've had a favorite four letter word: MORE. For some reason, accepting what I have at any particular moment has never been quite satisfying enough. If we had a great dinner, then I'd like seconds, please. If I was going to be involved in one activity, well, why not add in three or four more for good measure? And, frankly, it's a good thing I started having children later in life and nature (and exhaustion) stopped me at just three.

This "more" mentality has wormed its way over into my sense of self as well. I was not content to be on the student council; I had to be a class officer. I couldn't merely graduate, I had to graduate with honors. This compulsion to achieve, to be "MORE" has, in many respects, given me skills I might not have acquired. Those skills have served me well and allowed me, for example, to take on leadership roles. But I also am finding that my "MORE" ethic has, at times, had an opposite outcome and has held me back. For instance, I have a love of theater and would dearly love to be involved in it. I happen to live in a town rich in opportunities for such involvement. But where does my mind go? Theater? Well, why bother with Community Theater when there's Broadway? And of course, that is futile, so then, why bother? If I can't be at the top, in my mind, the effort to become involved in theatre just doesn't seem worth it.

Life, in its inimitable way, has been giving me many lessons in humility of late, along with the ability to see, and be present and grateful for where I am and what I am doing in the moment, regardless of what might be. As the Zen proverb states, "Before enlightenment; *chop wood, carry water.* After enlightenment; *chop wood, carry water.*" There is honor and integrity in a job well done, regardless of its nature.

And yet, there remains this niggling voice inside of me that keeps urging me to be BIG. To make things BIGGER. I daydream of starting another company and immediately think of how to make it national. This in itself is not bad, but when it takes me too far from the present, or actually prevents me from being my optimal self NOW, it is detrimental. I recently voiced this concern to a trusted adviser who, in her simple, straightforward way, made it clear to me: the bigness I desire is not outside of me. The bigness exists within me. The urging I hear is that of my soul to recognize and accept me – ALL of me.

This simple message made me stop on my proverbial hamster track. I realized that all of my life I HAVE been looking outside of myself for recognition and validation, and although I thought I had acknowledged that behavior and righted my course, evidently I had neglected a piece of that work. I neglected to take the time to recognize that there is only one Janet MacMeekin Neal, a role of Broadway proportions, and that I am fulfilling it very, very well.

Now, do you think I could get a Tony for that?

Gray is Good Enough

YESTERDAY'S SNOW WAS JUST perfect. It drifted softly down and sugar-coated the trees, somehow avoiding the street. As I drove through the wintery wonderland, I was awed by the majesty of the scenery. What would make it even better, I thought, was a crystal blue sky.

Today the sky was crystal blue and the sun was reflecting wildly off that new carpet of white snow. It made you shield your eyes as soon as you stepped outside. "If only it wasn't so bright," was the thought running through my head.

Now, as I look out my window, I see that the usual gray clouds have taken over that blindingly blue sky. As the thought, "Oh, if only the blue sky were back," came drifting into my consciousness, I finally saw the absurdity of my thoughts. I suffer from a perpetual need for perfection and for "more." The concept of "good enough" is nearly a foreign idea to me. If I am like this with the scenery around me, you can only imagine how I am with myself! And my poor children! It's a constant balancing act in learning how to acknowledge the positive, and encourage growth and expansion, without coming across as continually focusing on the negative.

When I watch the Olympics, I am always interested in observing not only the athletes, but their coaches. I can guarantee that while they were pumping up their prodigies prior to their events, they also were pointing out what could be improved upon after their performances were complete. The desire for continual improvement is a quality necessary in order to compete, but when does it become too much?

As much as Bode Miller can drive me nuts due to his off-the-slope antics, I actually think he may have figured part of this out. After a silver medal-winning Olympics ski run, he took a moment before looking at the results. Later, in an interview, he explained that before he looked at the scoring, he went inside himself to see how his performance felt to him. Content with his run, and believing that he had done all that he could have, he then looked, and learned that he had missed gold by only 9/100's of a second. And, although disappointed, he told the interviewer that he really was OK, because he had done all that he could and, he said, it was good enough. He was secure with the answer within.

For the rest of the day I am going to look at my life through the lens of "good enough." I'm going to dismiss the thoughts of needing to do, or be, more. I'll learn to accept the beauty in myself and in that which is surrounding me. Maybe I'll even learn to appreciate a gray winter day.

What's It Worth to You?

I LOVE FINDING PATTERNS in seemingly incongruent items. There is something very rewarding about being able to see the invisible thread that ties things together. The process is very satisfying, that is, unless it ends up revealing something akin to looking in the mirror.

I was sharing with my friends from grad school three recent stories from my life: one about work, one about my family, and one about my relationship. These women and I have known each other for a few years now and we touch base monthly to catch up on each others' lives and to offer a listening ear, a shoulder to cry on or a shared laugh. In my case, they have become my Emotional Advisory Board (EAB). They are able to hear what I can't hear, see what I can't see, and have the courage to say what I can't or won't say. I highly recommend having an EAB of your own! In this particular scenario, my EAB pointed out the invisible thread running through all the stories: value. They noted that, of course, these stories were not about the other people valuing me, but really raised the question of how I value myself. That statement created its own seismic activity within me.

I've been pondering this idea of how I value myself for a week now. To be honest, it's a tough exercise. What I have come to realize is that, upon awakening each morning, I strap on my protective ego in order to face the world. This protective garb is complete with a navigational guidance system that is finely tuned to pick up the reactions of all in my path, sending back instantaneous feedback to allow for course corrections at a moment's notice. I used to wear the heavy duty model that prevented any outside influences from seeing inside of me and provided a rather thick, protective skin. These days, I go for a more translucent version, but still with incredible sonar feedback systems. My value, therefore, is based on the information these systems receive and report back to me.

Following my EAB's feedback, I decided to try on, as an experiment, a different scenario. What if I DIDN'T put on the ego armor? What a totally scary proposition! But I went through with the visualization, if for no other reason than curiosity. First of all, when imaging myself without that emotional body armor, I felt incredibly light and free. It was a feeling counterintuitive to what I "knew" would happen if I let it go. Next, when I asked myself the question, "How do I value myself?" while in that armorless state, I nearly laughed. There was no need for the question: I simply was. I was good enough as is.

I wish I could say that that imagery was all I needed to put my ego armor in mothballs. I'm not quite there yet. But I feel like I've "seen the light" and it's not terribly scary. It may even be the easier, softer way to go. One of these days I'll surprise myself and let the armor go. I think, that in the process of doing so, I just may find that I'm worth it.

Never Enough

THERE'S A STORY ABOUT a man of great faith who was waiting on his roof for God to come and rescue him from the floods. He sent away the rescuers in the rowboat saying, "God will save me". He sent away the helicopter saying, "God will save me." Finally the flood waters overpowered him and he awoke in Heaven, sitting in front of God. "I don't get it, God," the man said. "I had great faith that you would save me and look where I ended up!" God answered, "I don't get it either. I sent you a rowboat and a helicopter..." Somehow I feel I'm relating to that man a little too much.

I don't know why I feel like I'm merely treading water these days, just biding my time until I can start to do what I'm REALLY supposed to be doing in this life. All this reconnection with my past of late has left me with the attitude of "Well sure I made a difference back then, but what am I doing now?" I can picture the conversation right now with God: I've arrived at the Pearly Gates and am feeling so sad that I didn't accomplish my mission. "What about your children?" he'll ask.

"Oh, yes, well, I did the best I could. Look what they've been able to do for themselves!"

"Well, what about your work? The people you helped launch and grow their businesses? The ones who re-examined their lives because of your workshops and writings?"

"I'm truly grateful for that. But I never got to really be of service!"

"And what about the Sunday School teaching, the tutoring, the PTAs, the committee work, the boards, the carpooling? What about the times you were there for a friend? What was all that?"

"Yes, yes, yes. But it wasn't ENOUGH!"

At that point I picture God throwing up his hands, shaking his head and walking away muttering under his breath.

OK, maybe I'm just where I'm supposed to be. At least for today.

Taking the Costanza Test

I NEVER TAKE THOSE ridiculous quizzes on Facebook. In fact, I teach courses on how to use Facebook where I advise people not to take them, as they merely are ploys for advertisers to gather your data and data about your friends. So I never take them. Except for the ones of value, or if I'm really bored. And wouldn't you know, there was a quiz on the Myers Briggs Personality Test just at the time I was a little bored. Never say never.

I have taken a plethora of personality tests in my day. Generally, by the time the test giver is handing me the packet, they already have determined that I am an extrovert. I guess I don't hide that trait too well. But lest I may have changed in the last few days, I took the test anyway. And sure enough, it came back with the same glaring result: extrovert extraordinaire. Shortly after taking the test I was in a meeting where I heard someone explaining yet another way to determine if you are an extrovert or an introvert: an extrovert will get energized being in a group, whereas an introvert will feel drained by the same experience. Working out of my home office for hours, and sometimes days on end, actually does have a draining effect on me, but get me in front of an audience for a presentation and I am ready to go! No denying my personality type!

With personality types in mind, I have stumbled upon a good way to determine the state of being of a person's self-esteem. We'll call it the "Costanza Test," based on the *Seinfeld* episode where George Costanza did everything the opposite of what he normally would– and for him it had remarkably good results. With this test, you do the opposite of what you would normally do, based on your personality type. So if you are an extrovert, don't talk to anyone. If you are an introvert, talk to a lot of people. And then, after about 24 hours, see how you feel.

I did this social experiment when I went on a retreat and decided to be silent for 24 hours. Not so easy to do when 1) everyone else is talking, 2) no one really knows what you are doing, and 3) you are an extrovert extraordinaire. What happened was my realization that I didn't know how to be silent in a group (Do you avoid eye contact? Risk being considered rude?) and that I REALLY rely on the feedback of others to determine how I am doing. In other words, on the Costanza Test scale of 1 being low self esteem and 10 being high, I was down around a 3. Fortunately I had a couple of days more to reverse my low score and, by the time I left, I was back up to about an 8: still preferring to be around others and still liking the attention, but definitely not feeling the NEED to have it in order to feel good about myself. I only can imagine how the opposite would be true if I were an introvert: that after being around others, I would learn that I am (or can be) OK wherever I am. Not that I can imagine being an introvert…

Regardless of your personality type, what resides inside remains the true barometer of, and testament to, your well-being. An introvert can no more imagine loving standing up in front of a crowd than I can imagine loving being alone for hours on end. But how you feel inside when you are doing those things really makes the difference. Take some time to recognize it and if need be, repair it. Hey, maybe there's a Facebook quiz to help you do that too…

Janet M. Neal

Thoughts on Being Fearless

ANNE LAMOTT IS ONE of my favorite authors. Her words are luscious and her descriptions of her life and experiences are both heartbreakingly honest and hysterically funny. So when I saw that she was going to be a speaker at a conference in New York sponsored by the Omega Institute – one of my favorite authors in one of my favorite cities sponsored by one of my favorite places AND on my birthday – well, I just figured it was meant to be. I knew that seeing Anne would be a pretty good present to give myself. What I found, though, was that she actually turned out to be the bow on the top of a box of wisdom and inspiration gifted to me by the other speakers.

My first gift was one of awareness of just how much I have conformed to my environment. Iyanla Vanzant was leading the first workshop I attended. If you've never heard her, she is dynamic. She also wears all white flowing gowns and started the class by having everyone dance. Right. At 8:30 a.m. on a Saturday in New York City?! Now, had this been eight months ago when I was still in school in California, I probably wouldn't have minded, nor thought anything about it. It was interesting to see how quickly I had morphed back into a cynical east-coaster!

Next, by accident, I got a gift of learning another lesson. I had misread the conference program and thought that the events on Friday evening were all part of an optional pre-conference intensive, which required a separate fee. But when I heard people buzzing on Saturday morning about Mia Farrow's emotional talk the night before on her work in Darfur, I quickly realized that I had blown it! My gift was the opportunity to practice self-forgiveness and to learn to stay in the moment – both of which I was finding hard to do. I found my mind drifting during other speakers' presentations as I wondered how her talk had been, what else I had missed and how could I have been so dumb as to have misread the program. This mistake seemed to be a gift that kept on giving!

The conference was entitled "Being Fearless" and speaker after speaker emphasized that fear is nothing to ignore or to run from, but to embrace and move through. Each presenter emphasized that we all have fear, and when we can release the stories we carry about it, we can become the powerful, amazing people who are just waiting to emerge from within. An analogy Noah benShea told illustrated this lesson so well for me: Suppose you had 12 horses that had to carry all your faith and your fears. If 11 of these horses carried your fears and only one had your faith, which would you put in front? You wouldn't want any of the 11 to lead – they would go nowhere. But if you put that one horse with faith in front, it would lead the others on the way.

I heard Reverend Michael Beckwith proclaim that vision without action is fantasy and that action without vision is chaos. I heard Robert Kennedy Jr. give example after example of the travesties of justice relating to, and mutilation of, the environment occurring in the US today and how he was at the same time, shocked, horrified, and inspired to take action. I heard Zev Kadash share a moving and unbelievably terrifying, true story of his experience as a child in a concentration camp where he was one of the Jews on "Schindler's List" and how he was awed by the strength of the human spirit to survive.

In short, I was totally inspired and ready to sell all my earthly possessions, move to a commune, eat only organic, raw foods and meditate for hours on end – all with a smile on my face and love in my heart.

And then Carolyn Myss, in her irascible, no-nonsense manner, said something that shocked me back to reality. She said that what you don't want to do is to keep searching for your purpose. What you want to do is to ask to wake up and be madly in love with the people in your life and where you are in life. It is the old adage of not having what you want, but wanting what you have. And by doing so, you move through the fear and distractions into your being.

I realized just how masterful I am at creating distractions to the avoid facing fear in my life. I'll start another project, another hobby, another relationship – anything to avoid having to stay put and address the fear. And I also saw how rich and powerful my life is, and can be, if I could learn to live it fully.

Anne Lamott concluded the conference with some words on everyday courage that gave me both pause and laughter. Following her talk, she was signing books and I got the chance to meet her and wish her a happy birthday, as she had shared that hers had been a couple days earlier. When I told her that it was my birthday too, and this conference was a gift to myself, she commented that there are a lot of powerful people born around this time. I smiled, and knew in my heart that I was, indeed, one of them.

Batting .500

BEING A BASEBALL FAN, I know that if you bat .500, you are doing really, really well. My grandfather, Harry E. Potter (yes, he is the REAL and ORIGINAL Harry Potter, without the lightning bolt scar and wizardry, of course), was a semi-pro baseball player who, one season, batted .500. An admirable accomplishment and one rarely attained. So why doesn't this sense of pride in doing half of something really well translate into other aspects of life?

Take today, for instance. I had four things on my To Do list: 1) get through my pile of pending items on my desk, 2) do the usual core things: meditate, exercise, write, 3) compose my Christmas letter, and 4) mail Christmas packages. By day's end I had batted .500, but somehow, I'm not feeling very proud.

Part of the problem is my level of expectation. I expect that I should get through the pile of things to do, lumping them all into one category. The reality is, that there were at least three items in there that took significant time to complete. So, if I wanted to, I could cut myself some slack and acknowledge that I REALLY accomplished far more than four things today!

My challenge is either to be more realistic with my goals (I thought four items were doable but perhaps that was the optimist in me talking...) or to learn to congratulate myself on all that I DID accomplish. Either would work, but I have a feeling that if I concentrated on the latter it would help me a bit more overall.

Or maybe learn to be happy with .500. Right.....

No Autographs, Please

I swear I saw George Stephanopoulos on the elliptical machine at the Y this morning. He even smiled at me the third time I looked at him – a sure sign I was correct. Well, at least that's the story I'm sticking with today.

I happen to live in an area where some celebrities also reside. Seeing one at the Y, or the grocery store, or at a soccer game is not terribly uncommon. But I can't understand why I, like so many others, still get a little thrill when a "sighting" takes place. I mean, really, would I get that excited about seeing someone ask the clerk if they had octopus today if it were anyone other than Stephen Colbert? I highly doubt it.

The other day, two very energetic and socially minded young men came to my door to encourage me to join their campaign against the government buying animal-grade meat to use in school lunch programs (sad but true). We had a great conversation and I was admiring their dedication to making the world a better place. As we wound up our conversation, they had one final question: Where do the celebrities live around here? I assured them that, after meeting me, the rest would be downhill. Somehow I don't think they believed me.

Today I'm going to carry myself in the stature of a celebrity. Maybe I'll even wear shades, even though it's not sunny. And it's not about getting the attention (although I never mind that!), but more about believing that I am worth it. No autographs, please...

Chapter Four
Loving What You Do and Doing What You Love

Choosing Gratitude

I AM CHOOSING TO look back at the past year with gratitude. Oh sure, there were personal setbacks and disappointments, the dramas of teen and pre-teen children, the trauma of exploding water pipes, and the frustration of lost business deals. It would be easy to get caught up in the negativity of those things. But for me, life is too short. I need the benefits that gratitude can give.

It has long been recognized that approaching life with an attitude of gratitude does wonders for the spirit. Experts also have acknowledged that such an attitude has benefits for the body as well as the soul. We are energetic beings and having positive energy flow within and around us strengthens the immune system. Conversely, negative energy blocks the flow of energy through various parts of our bodies and weakens the immune system, making us more prone to illness.

This theory was borne out in research conducted by Michael McCollough of Southern Methodist University in Dallas, and Robert Emmons of the University of California, Davis. Drs. McCollough and Emmons conducted a research project on gratitude and thanksgiving. Their findings scientifically proved that those who practice on-going gratitude, both for what they have and for what others do for them, have higher levels of alertness, enthusiasm, determination, optimism and energy. They also found that it was optimism that served to boost the immune system.

In addition to the health benefits, having and expressing gratitude provides a strengthening of morale, and spiritual values. As the late Ardath Rodale once said regarding gratitude, "It signals a healthy respect for other people; it shows an understanding of the difference between one's wants and needs; it clarifies that most things in life are privileges, not rights; it acknowledges the value of time and effort." Gratitude and thanksgiving provide, not only benefits to those giving, but to those on the receiving end as well. And, considering life today, there are not too many things about which you can make such a statement!

How can I start to reap these benefits? I can begin by starting to say "thank you" more often – to my partner, my children, my friends, my coworkers – anyone that does something for me. Those little words, said sincerely and with a smile, can start a positive-energy chain reaction! Another way that I can express my gratitude is to send handwritten "Thank you" notes to show people for whom I am grateful that I really care.

Another wonderful thing I do is to compose a daily gratitude list. I end each day by listing five to ten things I was grateful for that day. Besides becoming a wonderful chronicle of my life, my list serves as an attitude-shifter as well. If I am consciously looking for things throughout the day for which to be grateful, I won't be focusing on the negative.

I'm looking back on the past year with gratitude. I sent out a huge thank you to those who have given me support, both personally and professionally. I know I am better for it.

On Being 93

I went to visit my dear aunt on her 93rd birthday. What a treat it was, indeed, as I truly had thought that the next time I traveled to her home would be for her funeral. She had been very ill but now has rallied to a point where it was not easy to tell that she had ever been at death's door. The light shone brightly from her eyes and made her look more alive than others whom I've seen who were lifetimes younger than she.

I can't imagine what it must be like to be 93 any more than I could imagine, when I was a child, what it would be like to be 53. I'm actually *still* trying to figure out what growing older means, even though I've had a couple years of practice at it now. I wonder if, when you are 93, you still think you're a 19-year-old trapped inside an unfamiliar body, like I do today. I wonder if you stare at yourself in the mirror and see your parents' faces. I wonder if you still look ahead to what will be, or if you finally realize that… this is it.

When I'm 93, I hope I am still of sound mind, body and spirit. I hope I am surrounded by those I love, but if I'm not, I hope I still recognize my loved ones when I do see them and remember just what I love about them. I hope I can walk in the sunshine, but if I can't, I hope I can sit and appreciate the spring breeze and the smell of budding life about to burst anew. I hope I can share a conversation and a laugh with friends, but if I can't, I hope I can remember the times I did.

I hope, for today, that I can live fully and appreciate what an amazing life I've got, so that when I am 93, I'll have wonderful memories to keep me smiling.

On Being a Conduit...

ONE OF THE MORE lofty and heartfelt goals in my life is to be a conduit for the goodness of the Universe. The thought of being a messenger of "Divine Directives" just gives me goosebumps. I have worked hard to learn to both quiet my mind to "hear" those directives and then to trust my intuition when I "feel" them. And it was during a recent meditation that I was gifted with an awareness about this whole concept of "conduits".

Whenever I hear the word "conduit" I immediately flash to PVC piping. I believe that this mental leap comes from years of remodeling houses and living with exposed PVC piping for many of those years. The concept is very simple – a tubular device allows some type of substance to pass through, creating a direct line to a destination. There are three aspects to the use of the conduit: the input, the passageway and the output. Got it – or so I thought.

I realized that, as I said before, I've worked to perfect my *input* by getting myself into a position to receive. I've read that these divine messages are kind of like radio waves: they are constantly swarming around us, invisible and unrecognizable to most, and it is only with the right receiver that you can pick them up. And not all receivers will pick up the same waves/ messages, just like you can't access AM signals if you have an FM receiver. (Or perhaps I am dating myself and should say "HD vs. non-HD"...) Anyway, through meditation, and other self-awareness vehicles, I have learned to "receive" some messages, although most times it shocks me when I actually do. And in regards to the output, through all of my teaching, coaching and training of others, I have learned to deliver a message pretty well. I just realized, however, from one of those "shocking" messages that I've recently received, that maybe I am not quite so great at the middle part of the process.

It all boils down to this: if I'm going to be the mouthpiece, perhaps I need to remember that it's the MESSAGE that's important, not me. I came to realize that many times I'll get an idea/message, and then sit on it and I try to figure out what to do with it. As in, how do I put the right spin on it? But thinking about that PVC example, I don't seem to recall any piping taking in a substance, deciding what the outcome *really* should be, and then spitting it out. I am not sure why I feel that I need to massage the message to make it seem more...what? Pretty? Acceptable? Interesting?

On rare occasions, I have allowed myself to simply be the conduit, and it always surprised me when the person on the receiving end knew what I was imparting, even when I did not. I recall how I mentioned a single word to a client just once because I couldn't get the word out of my head. Of course I had to apologize in advance to save face, just in case she thought I was totally bizarre. But she absolutely knew what that single word was about and thanked me profusely for my help. Still, to this day, I have no idea how that strange but important communication happened, but I am grateful that it did.

My writing is really my attempt to strengthen the "middle part" of the conduit process. Without feedback from my readers, I have no clear idea as to whether others find meaning in my thoughts and messages, but somehow, when I receive ideas, I feel compelled to write them down, to be a conduit. Not being able to see my readers' faces to sense whether my messages have been delivered clearly does shield my ego a bit, but it is good practice for me to learn to trust my instincts and move forward on my path, PVC piping and all.

The 30 Year Gift

It has been said that the best things come to those who wait. I'm finding that sometimes the gifts can take as long as 30 years to arrive: I just got a note from one of my former students!

Thirty some years ago I was a bright-eyed, dark-haired, exuberant optimist who could not WAIT to be a teacher. I had known since I was in first grade that this is what I would do and it seemed like an eternity until I could actually fulfill the dream. When I graduated from college there was a glut of teachers and very few jobs. My parents and other worried relatives and adult family friends, tentatively asked me what I was going to do. "Get a teaching job!" was my reply. I was confident that there was one out there for me, regardless of how long it could take or where I had to move. I did a lot of substituting and waitressing until a teaching job came through, just as I knew it would. I was finally on my path!

A new elementary school had opened in Lapeer, Michigan and I was hired to teach a combination 3rd and 4th grade class. I can still feel that sense of pride and excitement in setting up my classroom for the first time. The only issue was the classroom itself. Following the best of educational intentions, one wing of the school had been designed to accommodate the latest teaching trend: open classrooms. The theory behind this absence of structure was, that by eliminating physical walls, it encouraged and enabled children to move freely to the areas in the building where the most level-appropriate training for them was available. Great idea, bad execution. Basically, what was done was to build a traditional school wing without installing any walls. You can imagine the noise issues and chaos created by having six classrooms of 8-to-12-year-olds all able to hear and see each other at all times. I believe it was about day two of the school year when the portable chalk boards came rolling in to create, at least visual, barriers.

In addition to the physical space challenges that year, I also was "gifted" with a class of 29 children with no aide. And, being the rookie, I also was allowed to experience all of the children that the other 3rd grade teacher didn't want to handle. I was up for the challenge and loved each unique personality – and believe me, we had them! I spent many hours coaxing Superman off the desk, the shy one out from under the table, and holding the nervous ones until they were brave enough to go to gym class. Somewhere in there I must have taught them something too – or at least tried to. It was draining, and exasperating at times, but it also was fun and, at the outset, I wouldn't have traded a minute of it.

I left the elementary classroom four years later feeling absolutely wiped out. It was one of the more discouraging times in my life. I had known that I was a teacher at heart, and yet my "dream job" was, after the initial excitement, making me physically sick. It was just too much for me and I left the education arena for what started as a summer job in the corporate world, and never returned to the classroom. However, even though I was out of education, I still considered myself a teacher, which resulted in a big mismatch in my self-concept and a feeling that, somehow, I had stepped away from my purpose in life.

Years passed and I left the corporate world for that of entrepreneurship. I was giving workshops I'd created entitled "How To Find Balance In Your Life," – a topic I'd learned about the hard way – and, invariably, at the completion of my presentation a few of the participants would come up to me and thank me, telling me that what I had presented was invaluable to them. It was probably after about the third time that this happened that it hit me: I'm teaching! I had had it set in my mind for so long that being a teacher meant having a classroom of children, that I had shut out any other possibilities of what teaching could mean. It was a spiritual awakening of sorts to realize that, YES! I am on my path after all.

It is so easy to go through my day without giving myself any credit for what I do or what I have done. I take it for granted that I'll use my skills and abilities and am actually quite harsh on myself when I don't feel that I've done a particular job to the best of my ability. After leaving teaching, I harbored some lingering thoughts that, although I think I did the best that I could at the time, it was, perhaps, not enough.

And then I got the note from JoEllen.

How she found me I am not sure, but yesterday, there in my inbox, was a brief note asking me if I was the Miss MacMeekin who used to teach 3rd grade. I immediately recognized the name and replied. She went on to say that she remembered me and told me I was the BEST teacher. I think I still have, tucked away in some storage box, those same words written in a 3rd grade girl's scrawl on a handcrafted card complete with hearts and rainbows and flowers. I know that her words are forever written in my heart. If I ever had any doubts that I am on the right path, I certainly don't have them now. What a beautiful gift, 30 years later!

The Other Side of the Equation

I WAS ALMOST A math major in college. Today, that thought boggles my mind! But I think my motivation came not so much from my love of the subject, as it did from the realization, now, that my best teachers were my math teachers – who taught me a lot more than just math.

Although I distinctly recall all my math teachers, my favorite was Miss Laugginger. Her timed tests at the beginning of each class brought out my competitive spirit, once again making me want to prove that I was smarter than any boy in my class, particularly Ben Doot or Larry Laskey. (And, I might add, I think I proved that nicely, thank you very much...) Then there were the usual "trains leaving Chicago or San Francisco at different times" nonsense I could care less about. But what really got my attention was what happened in one particularly hormonal class session.

I can't recall all the details, but evidently there had been some sort of not-so-witty-repartee going on between students and, while I don't remember who said what, I remember *vividly* Miss Laugginger's reply, "Be careful what you say. It's a fine line between love and hate." And with that, she launched into a lecture on the subject, complete with a mathematical illustration of a circle, with a line through it, with love on one side of the line and hate on the other. She kept saying "Love and hate are not opposites – they are mirror emotions and it only takes a little bit to step over that line." I had no idea what she was talking about.

Years, and many chances to experience that lecture firsthand later, I understand what Miss Laugginger was trying to teach us. Passion is a fiery emotion which easily can go on either side of that thin line. The true opposite of passion is no emotion at all. With all the emphasis on bullying of late, the TV show *Glee* had an interesting story line wherein the openly gay character was being bullied by the big brute football player...who then turned out to be secretly gay himself. To paraphrase Shakespeare, "Methinks thou dost protest too much."

In today's supercharged, highly passionate environment, it is easy to get caught up in judgments against others and fall into the negativity of gossip and name-calling. But if we are feeling so much passion on the topic, aren't we just that much closer to "the other side" of the equation? I think Miss Laugginger would agree with me on this one.

The Power of Bamboo

I ALWAYS WANTED A bamboo plant for my office: I heard they brought good luck. But I also heard that they brought good luck IF they were presented as a gift. So, for that reason, I never bought one. And I never got one, which annoyed me to no end because really, shouldn't people be able to read my mind by now?

So I was absolutely thrilled upon receiving a very late Mother's Day present of a little bamboo shoot. It just happened to coincide with my taking a new job, so of course I took the arrival of the gift as a good omen. It is now sitting proudly on my desk, rightfully claiming its place in my "wealth corner." Not that I am superstitious or anything, but hey...

I was watching an interview with John Isner, the American tennis player who had been in an unbelievably long tennis match. This interview was prior to his next match, and he was asked if he has a typical routine that he goes through before a match. He said that he did, but that he was going to alter it a bit because of the circumstances. I was shocked! Most athletes I've seen are THE most superstitious people and have to go through their same routine – or else! Did you ever see Nomar Garciaparra before coming to bat? Yikes! Anyway, I thought that maybe young John was not too smart to be changing things up at this point in his career and couldn't help but feel a little sorry for him. Poor kid – he probably was going to lose.

Well, evidently, the joke was on me. He won! So now I think I'll take a minute and revisit my ideas on superstitious routines. Maybe I'll even stop giving my little bamboo plant so much power over the success in my life and start believing that my achievements might have something to do with me.

It still was a nice gift though...

Passion + Baseball = Steinbrenner

I USED TO BE one of those people who hated George Steinbrenner. And I knew I had lots of company. He was obnoxious and overbearing and so over-the-top full of himself. Then I became a New York Yankees fan and I tempered that feeling a bit – but only a bit. Only in the past few years, since his death in 2010, have I been able to see that the man's passion was the all-important key in turning around a failing team and resurrecting a baseball dynasty. His passionate energy and vision not only saved an historic sports franchise, but extended into the greater New York community as well and, as the years go on, I am sure that I'll learn more and more about how the former owner of the New York Yankees touched people's lives.

So what can I learn about passion from this man? Well, for one, that emotion isn't always pretty. If you have it, it doesn't mean everyone will always like you, or agree with you. But it seems to be the rock that Steinbrenner relied on time and time again, and it also was what drove him, even when everyone around him had opinions contrary to his. He was the light-bearer in the team's dark times, even if that torch may have burned a few naysayers in its path. And it lit a few others' torches in the process.

I can't imagine myself ever being comfortable knowing that there are people who revile me – it's just not my personality. But I can learn to stand a little straighter and believe in my convictions, even in the face of adversity. I can learn to embrace my passions and pursue them wholeheartedly, knowing that there is nothing that can take them from me. And I can cheer on my Yankees again and again...thanks to a man who had a clear vision of their greatness! RIP George.

Start With the Gratitude

I CAN BEGIN WITH gratitude.

I didn't know what to write today. It had been a while – too long in fact. So much for my commitment to every day! It seemed as if my new job had snuck in and taken over my leisurely lifestyle. But today I had a few minutes before needing to dash off and I felt clear-headed and eager to write. The problem, though, was that I was too clear-headed. Blank, in fact. And as I sat there, dejectedly slumped in my chair staring at the computer screen, the words came to me: I can begin with gratitude.

I can begin by being grateful that I woke up without my usual, unfortunate headache this morning. That I didn't have to take the medicine that immediately takes away the pain but also makes everything else mushy - like trying to push through a bowl of oatmeal. I'm grateful for the large and ever-growing pile of work to do because it means that our staff is helping more people. And I'm grateful to have a clear head today to be able to handle my work.

I am grateful that the rain and wind have stopped and that there is a beam of sunlight peeking in my window with the promise of much more ahead. I am grateful that the gorgeous, enormous, elm tree in my yard, that got diseased and died earlier in the year, was removed so that it didn't end up in our house this weekend due to high winds. And I'm grateful that ours was one of the homes that didn't lose power, except for one hour during the day when we hardly noticed it. And I'm especially grateful for a fiancé who went out in the storm's fury to get me some dessert because I was not feeling great. I'll even forget the fact that he ate most of it. Perhaps there's some gratitude in that as well...

I could go on and on with things for which I am grateful this day, but was just struck with another thought: the storm has stopped. Inside and out. Evidently the pathway to peace does begin with gratitude.

Janet M. Neal

Calling Me Out

IT WAS THE THIRD invitation request that got me...the one that started "All right all you 'maybes' out there..." It's one thing to be non-committal, but it's quite another to be called out on it.

I have a love-hate relationship with Facebook's invitations to events. On the one hand, as an event provider, I love that Facebook offers a free service, and that I easily can invite everyone I know. As someone who gets countless invitations, however, I am not enamored with the fact that I get invited to things that are of no interest to me, or are geographically impossible to attend. I do, however, like that I can answer "attending," "ignore" or "maybe." If I definitely am not interested in an event, I ignore the invitation. If I don't want to hurt their feelings, I say "maybe." I figure I can hide out there, showing that I really did look at it and perhaps I *may* think about actually attending, that is, if I remember, and if nothing else comes up. It seems that with today's event I was "found out" and forced to take a stand.

I have been known to be a fence-straddler from way back. Never one to rock the boat or cause any controversy, I have been pretty happy being middle-of-the-road. I've been fairly secure in this behavior until this afternoon, after the above-mentioned event (which I DID attend and did enjoy, I might add). I was working on pulling together some old writing pieces for a friend and came across some poetry I had written when I was 15-years-old. I expected to revisit some lyrical ramblings about love, and instead found pretty strong position statements on war and peace, poverty, and pollution. Was there a strong radical living inside this Midwestern milquetoast all along? Perhaps all I needed was to be called out on it.

I still care what others think of me and probably still censor myself too often. But if I can conjure up that teenage passion every now and again, who knows where it may lead me?

(and just for fun....here's one of my poems:)

"Freedom Land" by Jan MacMeekin
America is
strong and proud
standing straight
back erect
apple pie and mom
freedom
Old Glory
blowing free
in the polluted
air to the
tune of broken
heads and
pleading cries
of the poverty stricken
America,
"land of the free
and home of the
brave" -
Live up to your name.

Janet M. Neal

Finding Your Inner Rudolph

I'VE DECIDED THAT RUDOLPH was really an ordinary reindeer who had a very bad cold. This makes him even that more admirable, considering that he not only went to work on a moment's notice, but pulled a sleigh, (OK, with a little help from his friends), at 30,000 feet above the earth, loaded with an overweight guy and enough presents for every kid in the world. I am definitely not a Rudolph.

I have come to this conclusion after catching a glimpse of myself in the mirror between sneezing fits and noticing that my once cute little schnoz has now taken on more of a WC Fields complexion. Cute is definitely not a word that would remotely describe it now. Neither would it describe my demeanor. I may have the nose of the esteemed reindeer, but I certainly am not sporting his winning and willing spirit! Instead of reveling in the joy of the holiday season, I am wallowing in self-pity. My inner child is alive and well and throwing a major, "It's not fair!" tantrum. As I sit home alone on day three of what was supposed to be a romantic snowed-in weekend, I am surrounded by boxes of tissues and every over-the-counter drug and homeopathic remedy I could find. My thrill of the weekend was sitting in a steam room at the YMCA.

But back to Rudolph... I remember as a kid reading our circa 1939 version of the story and being struck by three things: 1) How creepy the pictures were, 2) How mean the other reindeer were to Rudolph, and 3) How Santa never really seemed to care about him until he needed him. (Perhaps I did have a bit of cynicism brewing in me at an early age....) Reading the tale today, I still think that the pictures are creepy and so are the other reindeer, and I'm still not too thrilled with Santa's not standing up sooner for Rudolph. But there is another take I have on this. I am seeing Rudolph in a whole new light, if you'll excuse the pun. Here's a guy saddled with something that made him an outsider, with seemingly no one there helping to make things "OK" for him. He tries to fit in by attempting to cover up his "uniqueness" but that doesn't work and he's left feeling worse than ever. And then, that moment comes, when he is given the opportunity to use what he had thought of as his curse as a gift. And better yet, he sees how, by using his gift, he can truly serve others. He may have a gift, but it really is not an asset until he shares it.

I still struggle with feeling like I need to figure out what my "gift" is. This weekend, I found out that it definitely is not being a compassionate person when sick! I still harbor a belief that my gift needs to be huge and significant, and yet I see daily reminders that what makes a difference really are the little things: clerks at Whole Foods singing along to the holiday soundtrack piped throughout the store and putting a smile on my face; getting a note from an across-the-country friend wishing me well; or even receiving a simple text message, sent merely to remind me that I am loved.

May you find your "Rudolph moment," blessing others with the unique gift of you!

(PS....After telling my daughter about this article she basically told me I'd better watch out (better not cry?), and to "stop hating" and start sending Santa some love! I went back and re-read the book (pictures still creepy), but discovered that, according to this version, Santa didn't know Rudolph existed until he went to fill his stocking! Therefore, it was the 1960s TV version of the Rudolph story that gave the apparently inaccurate and unfortunate portrayal of Santa knowing of the abuse and doing nothing about it. I stand corrected, and beg the Big Man's forgiveness. Hopefully, there will be more than just coal in my stocking this year!)

Janet M. Neal

Rolling Out the Red Carpet

LIFE, AT TIMES, SEEMS so trivial to me. I step back and look at the "drama" around me in things such as children complaining that they have nothing to wear when their dresser drawers are so full that the bottoms literally are falling out, or in spending hours researching whether I should stick with my Blackberry or switch to the iPhone. There is little in the day-to-day that seems to matter in the grand scheme of things. I thought that perhaps it was time to look inside for some answers.

I began my 20-minute meditation as always, with deep cleansing breaths to take in the good and release that which I no longer needed. And I when I felt ready, I settled into a comfortable breathing pattern and cleared my mind and waited. That takes about two minutes. The following 16 minutes consisted of making lists of things I needed to do, and then catching myself, berating myself, forgiving myself for berating myself, and then starting the whole cycle all over again. Finally, with about two minutes left, I focused back on the original question du jour: What is life all about? Surely something I'd be able to figure out in my session's remaining time!

I reflected on a prior meditative session when the answer had come to me in stunning clarity: Love. That's what it was all about, that is why we are here. And before my cynical mind could jump in and run with the new revelation, a more willing part came forward and asked, "OK, so how do I do that?" The answer came back: "Use your gifts." I mused a bit as to what gifts I had and then said, "Well, I can write." "Then write," came the answer.

Again, I was perplexed. "But I don't know what to write!" I said. An image of a giant rolled carpet appeared in my mind and a voice said, "Do you trust me?" I answered, hesitatingly,

"Ah, yes," and the carpet unrolled a tiny bit. The voice said again, "Do you trust me?" This time I answered a bit more convincingly: "Yes," I replied. The carpet unrolled a bit more. One more time the voice came back: "But do you REALLY trust me?" I had to think about that one. Finally, I took a deep breath, exhaled, and said confidently, "Yes, I really trust you."

The carpet unfurled. It was red, like the ones the celebrities walk at the awards shows. I thought, "Oh, how cute, the red carpet is being rolled out for me." I was waiting for it to stop unfurling. But it didn't stop. It just went on, and on, and on, and on. I became aware that life's possibilities, like that carpet, were endless. I was awestruck. At that point I had the knowing that all I had to do was to use my gifts and life would be rolled out for me. There was nothing more that I had to do.

So, what did I do? Relax in gratitude? Finally exhale knowing that all would be OK? No – I started planning what I needed to do next. Me, myself – no divine inspiration/ intervention, thank you. That lovely red carpet? It immediately rolled back up. Ah....another lesson learned: Seems that taking back control negates all that good, insightful stuff.

The chime went off announcing that my meditation time was over. I wish I could say that I miraculously have been changed and that this wisdom has cured what ails me. What I can say though, is that although there are still annoyingly petty things in my life, like needing to pay bills or clean my desk, I know that if I make the time to do the things I'm good at, there's a wicked-long red carpet out there with my name on it!

Chapter Five
Life Through a New Lens

Spring in January

THE PERSON IN FRONT of me at the drive-thru ATM obviously was having some operator difficulty as she had now partially opened her door and was hanging out, trying to complete her banking transaction. The person behind me also was in some sort of distress, and was beeping his horn impatiently. I was in the luxurious position of having time on my hands, having had a meeting cancelled while I was en route to it. Between thinking, "What IS she doing up there?" and, "Could he be beeping at me? What does he want me to do, ram the car in front of me to get her to hurry up?," I just sat back and let my mind wander, grateful that the heater in my car was fully operational. Man, it was COLD!

A movement to my right caught my eye and I noticed a little bird hopping under some bushes. How sweet, I thought. It took a moment more before the whole scene registered: there was bright green grass, birds, sunlight....SPRING! Honestly, my heart fluttered. This little oasis had been carved out by the sunlight on the south side of the building, shielding it from the snow and other wintery effects. It was nothing short of magical to me and infused me with a large helping of hope that, in spite of the cold and dreariness enveloping us of late, signs of better times ahead could be found.

When I got home, still buoyed by warm and happy thoughts, I looked up at a tree in my yard. There, on the branches, were red leaf buds. No way. Didn't this tree know that it was 17 degrees outside?? I kept looking around to see if this was a joke, or, maybe I really had missed a couple of months along the way. I didn't find any other examples like it, but the fact of its existence stayed with me. It stood there, almost defiantly optimistic that yes, Spring IS on its way.

I'd love to be more like that tree – able to stand strong through adverse conditions and still offer a promise of better days ahead. Or like that bird who found that patch of sunshine in an otherwise gray world. Perhaps if I could do that, I might make the path a little brighter for someone else as well. Maybe even a harried ATM user.

Janet M. Neal

Yellow Roses and Stephen Colbert

A few Valentines Days ago I saw a news story on the meaning of the various colors of roses. Why that made the national news, I don't know, but of course I watched it. The only thing I remembered was that red was for true love and that yellow was for friendship. About that time I had started seeing my (now) fiancé, who has a wonderful habit of buying me flowers – roses in particular. I was joking with him about what he was trying to tell me through his choice of yellow ones and the "curse of the yellow roses" became a running joke with us. So it is understandable that, on Sunday when we were at the grocery store, I nearly missed my chance encounter with Stephen Colbert because of the yellow roses in our cart.

There are inherent dangers in having a degree in psychology. The good news is that I have a fascination with human behavior. The bad news is that I tend to spend WAY too much time analyzing situations and motivations, rather than taking them at face value. Here are my cases in point:

Situation one: Guy loves girl. Guy wants to show his love for said girl by buying flowers.

Situation Two: Couple is entertaining guests and goes to the grocery store for the supplies.

These are very mundane, normal situations, but I have been known to be able to make a Bic pen complicated. So here is how my analytic mind saw it:

Situation One: Guy loves girl. Guy wants to show his love for said girl by buying flowers. However, she has perfectly good flowers at home that he bought less than a week ago. Why does he feel the need to buy more? Is he feeling guilty for something? And then he picks out YELLOW ONES! Of course they are the prettiest and healthiest of the bunch, but really, yellow?! What is he really trying to tell her (me) here? Is this a joke or is it a subconscious message? And... the edges of the roses have a red tint to them. Does that change the situation?

You can see how, with these thoughts swirling in my head, I nearly missed Stephen Colbert brushing past me in the produce aisle. His wife had to ask me (very politely) to move. This jarred me out of my analysis and into a new one about situation two.

Situation Two: Couple entertaining and at the grocery store for supplies. Except the couple is made up of a celebrity who is acting rather standoffish. Is this because he doesn't want to draw attention to himself or because he is self-absorbed? And yet, his wife seems very warm and open. So what could I say that would get his attention in a non-threatening way and yet get him to see that I am a fascinating and funny person that yes, he'd love to have me on his show sometime. Or maybe even over for dinner. Heck, we're practically neighbors anyway. Although I'm not crazy about octopus, which is what he is trying to buy. I wonder how they cook that?

You get the picture...

My challenge today is to use my wonderfully analytical and creative mind to observe and move on – not to tie me down with worry and conjecture. I need to be grateful for what is, and not wonder about what could be. My reality today is that I am healthy and safe and have loving friends and family – and two, beautiful bouquets of roses on my table. Life is good, regardless of the color.

Janet M. Neal

Baseball's Been Bery, Bery Good to Me

I AM A LOYAL baseball fan. By that I mean that I am loyal to the team in the general vicinity of where I live. I grew up loving the Detroit Tigers. My allegiance shifted to the Red Sox when I lived in Boston. And ever since I moved to the New York City area in 1988, I've been a Yankees fan. These allegiances help out tremendously when confronted by situations like choosing a team to root for during the baseball season and, hopefully, also the World Series.

But what I love about baseball, regardless of which team is playing, is watching a team that is down for the count but never gives up. It gives me inspiration to see a group of individuals coming together, pulling for one another, and working for the common goal, without pausing to think about how impossible that may seem.

There are two teams that stand out for me as amazing examples of this: the 1998 NY Yankees and the 2004 Boston Red Sox. Dubbed the "anti-Yankees," Boston's '04, scruffy, mismatched-looking lot appeared, at first glance, to be anything but cohesive. But what their appearance belied was their unity of focus and dedication. Yes, they had a few key players, but their collective energy and belief in themselves is what propelled them to become that year's World Champions. (Yes, they beat my Yankees to get there, but see paragraph #1).

I've used the image of these teams to help keep me focused on my business goals. Whenever I got drubbed down, I would refocus on the goal. Instead of thinking "Why me?," I'd look at those amazing teams, whose superstars put their egos aside, shunned the spotlight, and played the game solely to help the teams win, and thought "Why not me?" And, yes, I was able to achieve my goals, just as they did. But without the tickertape parade.

Paulo Coelho, in his book, *The Alchemist*, notes that there are four obstacles to us attaining our goals:

1. Being told from childhood that you can't do it
2. Believing that if you achieve it, those you love will abandon you
3. Fear of the defeats you may encounter on your path
4. Fear of realizing the dream – feeling that you don't deserve it

Any one of these could be enough to scare you off. Look at the Red Sox – if they had listened to the critics (saying that they'd never do it), they wouldn't have. If the 1998 Yankees were afraid of losing, they would have given up time after time. And if either team's players had felt that they were unworthy of being world champs, they would have ended up as a bunch of minor leaguers.

The bottom line is acquiring an unwavering belief in yourself and your goal. If you can't do it by yourself, get someone to help you along the way: a coach, a friend...or a sports team for inspiration! And remember, if a hairy, Neanderthal-looking jock can become a sex symbol <u>and</u> a world champion, you just might have a shot at achieving your goal too!

Sky Mind

I read today in *Haiku Mind*, by Patricia Donegan, a verse written by poet Allen Ginsberg, which describes the concept of "sky mind." The Buddhist tradition of sky meditation says that, at any time, you can look into the sky to remember the vastness and openness that are always with us. I started thinking about that concept of my mind as the sky, with my thoughts and feelings merely clouds passing through, and realized the analogy works beautifully in my life.

In the morning, my mind is like the sky at sunrise: a bit of brightness trying to peak through, surrounded by a lot of fuzzy gray. Eventually, after moving around and having some coffee, the sky mind brightens and opens up. There are days when there are clouds – harmless, soft, fluffy, cumulus ones, like thoughts and feelings drifting in and out. Some days, there is even a wider expanse, as I am fully open to what the day may bring, with nothing to hold me back.

There are other days when, no matter what I do, there is fog. Maybe a light will shine through for a minute, but mainly, my thoughts are fuzzy. Some days the sky mind is dark and covered with angry clouds. Thoughts and feelings are intense and come fast and furiously. I need to remember that behind them is that beautiful, blue expansiveness, waiting patiently to make its presence known. This, too, shall pass.

The brightness of a spring day after a long, dull winter is nothing short of exhilarating to me…just like a day when my mind is clear and sharp and creative – a stark contrast to those foggy, muddled-mind days. With gratitude today, I gaze out my office window at the brightness greeting me and smile at the reminder of openness and possibility that life is presenting to me. The sky is, indeed, the limit.

Skating By

I'VE BEEN GOING OUT to California once a month for the past two years to attend graduate school. Most months I lug along my roller blades. There is a path along the beach in Santa Monica that is far too tempting to resist and I love being out in the sunshine, gliding along and viewing the magnificence of the broad beach and the rolling hills rising up from the sparkling ocean. Life is good and, suddenly, I am 19-years-old again. Dancing slightly to the tunes on my iPod, I smoothly maneuver past the more mundane who choose merely to walk.

And then I turn around to go back.

Suddenly, I have aged 30 years and feel and look utterly ridiculous. The path that seemed so flat a minute ago now has a slight, but VERY long, upgrade. Gliding is replaced with the desire just to keep moving and the hope of not falling. And those mundane people whom I passed before? They are now passing me.

That beach path is, to me, a reminder that life is not always easy, nor is it always hard. Some days the wind is at your back and what use to be difficult is now not so hard. Some days you feel your age, some days you are invincible. Some days you are pushing against the wind, knowing that this should be easy and wondering just where you went wrong.

I'm tempted, when I'm doing that long, uphill climb, to look at those gliding past in the opposite direction and exclaim "It's not fair!" I have a built-in selective memory mechanism which conveniently forgets that I was just there. It's easy to be so caught up in the pain of the moment that I don't see, that if I just turn around and go the other way, the journey would be much easier. It's interesting how easy it is

Janet M. Neal

to allow myself to get swept up in the "poor me's," which cuts me off from solutions that might make my life better!

When you're stuck on that path, raise your eyes a little higher and take in the bigger view. Getting your eyes off your problems may give you a chance to see something you might otherwise have missed. Changing your focus may just get you gliding again. And if nothing else, you'll start to feel cool again.

This Isn't Happening Just To Me?

I WAS AT A conference for women business leaders a couple of weeks ago listening to some very successful and respected women business owners talking about how to weather the economic storm. It must have been about a third of the way into the day when that little voice inside my head suddenly woke up and said, "You mean this isn't happening just to me?!" Now, I consider myself to be an intelligent woman with a relatively global perspective on life, but for some reason I was taking the economic downturn personally. As if forces conspired when they saw I was starting a business and said, "Ah, let's see how much she can really take!"

That realization makes me wonder what else I do that is wrapped up in that "it's all about me" thinking. Not that I'm asking for those who know me well to suddenly rush forward with substantiating evidence! And, unfortunately, I don't think that I'm alone in this phenomenon.

On the other side of that coin, whatever happens to one person affects the whole, even when it is good. We tend to focus on the negative, but what about positive trends? The Olympics are a great example. One person works very hard, achieves a goal and the country celebrates and shares in the pride and achievement. There are millions of little "wins" happening all over the world daily and we can be a part of those celebrations as well. Or, we can choose to focus on the losses and wallow in our victimhood.

I have seen these times become increasingly stressful and difficult for substantial numbers of people. I feel the fear that is oozing around us, eager to gain a foothold. And I have found myself sliding down that slippery slope into despair and gloom.

But I also have seen that there is a reawakening of the creative spirit. From the economic ashes I have seen amazing strength and ingenious solutions arise. I am feeling an energy that is gaining momentum, a shift from an "all about me" attitude, from being self-absorbed, to the holding out of hands to pull one another up. I have been infused with hope again and the prospect that, although the road may be rocky, we're still walking in the right direction.

When I reflect on all that I have, and that for which I am grateful, the realization that it is not all about me is one to rank high on my list. To realize that I am part of something much bigger and that together we have incredible resources to pull us through is, indeed, a blessing. I am grateful to all who, in their own ways, have pulled me up. May your path be full of extended hands as well.

A Joyful Martyr

I HAD JUST FINISHED telling my friend Leanne the long and sorry tale of the life decisions I've had to make in the past year and sat back to get her feedback. Her "Wow!" comment played nicely with my expectations, making me feel, ever-so-slightly, the justified martyr. Then she added "You sound so empowered! I also am feeling your joy. Where is the joy coming from?" Within about one second the following thoughts flashed through my mind: "What is she on?", "I think she's been living in the mountains too long", "Oh wow – her life is worse than mine", and, "Has she even been listening to me?"

Every so often a conversation or a phrase will serve as a virtual slap in the face to me: something that stops me in my tracks and wakes me to a different way of looking at the situation at hand. Leanne's comment did just that. It made me see my life through her eyes, instead of through the victim blinders I'd become so comfortable wearing.

I had described a situation of having to let go of a lot of things that were important to me, a forced simplification of life. Empowerment and Joy were not words I often (ever?) associated with letting go. I was too stuck in my story to see that, in making the decisions I'd made, I *had* taken back my power. I now have a lifestyle that works for where I am right now. And everything that is in it DOES bring me joy. I am not overly encumbered with "stuff" and am able to utilize my available resources on that which has value and meaning to me. Who knew?!

I once wrote, "Gratitude and Fear cannot live in the same place." If the absence of fear is empowerment, and gratitude = joy, I think Leanne is on to something! And I, for one, am grateful that she is.

Janet M. Neal

Bad Days and Mashed Potatoes

SOMEWHERE DURING MY TEEN years when I decided I was too fat (oh to be that "fat" again!), I gave up mashed potatoes. Not only did I not eat them, I convinced myself that I didn't even like the taste of them. There was no temptation any longer; eating mashed potatoes was just not something I did.

Having a "bad day" was also something that I just did not do any longer as of a few years ago. Unlike the mashed potatoes, I don't remember that change of behavior being a conscious decision on my part, but rather a new way of looking at life. It was how I was choosing to look at life, rather than letting circumstances dictate my mood. I really had a hard time imagining a day being "bad" – it became that foreign a concept to me.

It was the Blue Sky Restaurant that started the demise of my potato aversion. They had garlic smashed potatoes and since everyone raved about them, I had to try them. Let's just say that they were nothing like the milky whipped potatoes of my youth! Unfortunately, they hooked me back in and now...well, I'm salivating at the thought of them.

I'm not saying it's the mashed potatoes' fault, but I'm noticing that a few times in the past year I've also felt as though I was having a bad day. Nothing too serious, but the "I had a bad day" concept which used to be foreign to me, now has some degree of reality. And in the same way that "just one cookie" leads to a three month sugar binge for me, there's a danger in allowing myself to "have a bad day." Sure, some moments are not all that fun, but if I choose to see what I can learn from them, instead of starting to ladle on the self pity, the bad feelings dissipate much more quickly.

Holidays are awash with temptations and I know it's my choice on how I want to deal with them. A few potatoes here, a cookie there, a grouchy statement over here.... and the verbal "snowballs" will be flying in no time. Better to decide now that these will be the best days – and choose to really believe it. I know that I – and everyone around me – will be grateful for that decision!

Janet M. Neal

Costco and the Simple Things in Life

I HAVE FOUND THE trick to getting a teen who seemingly is tethered permanently to his video games, to leave his room: Take him to Costco.

I have tried all sorts of enticements in the past: shopping for new clothes, dinner at a favorite restaurant, or a walk in the park with the dog. Nothing seemed to work and I was pretty much at the point of accepting the fact that the days of my son being my little buddy were nothing but a sweet memory. So yesterday, when I stuck my head into his room to tell him that we were going to Costco – and then casually added, "Would you like to go?" I had absolutely NO expectation that there would be any interest, let alone any response! When he said "Sure!" I had to ask twice if he had really heard me correctly, and vice versa.

Back in the day when my kids were little, they certainly had their fair share of toys and games that they loved. But their favorite thing to play with was a big cardboard box from some kind of appliance. We had a great fort/playhouse on our porch for a while that they had fashioned from that box and in which they spent hours of imaginative play. The trip to Costco had a similar impact on my son. When he walked in, awed by the vastness and variety, he said, "If I ever had to be stuck in a store overnight, this would be the one I'd like to be stuck in." You could see the wheels turning on what an adventure that would be!

As my fiancé and I wandered around with my son and daughter, the kids were acting as if we had gone back in time about 10 years and they were in Toys R Us. I had to shepherd them away from the things we weren't there to buy and try to herd them toward the things we needed. Every corner held a new excitement: food samples! I swear, you'd think I never fed them. At one point I was waiting patiently for my two biological children while they stood in line to get pizza samples (the third "adult child" was off exploring and I gave up trying to corral him). My kids both looked over at me with excited little smiles and I swore, if I didn't know where we were, I would have thought that we were waiting for them to see Santa! Priceless!

I get so caught up in trying to figure out how to give my kids what they need, that I sometimes forget that their needs are really very simple. A warm home, a warm meal and a warm heart will probably give them most of what they require. My son's 17th birthday is coming up soon and I'm going to make sure I give him all those things…and maybe a trip to Costco and a cardboard box just to spice it up!

Janet M. Neal

Nature's Antidote

I SAW A HUMMINGBIRD yesterday.

I veered off of my usual morning routine of artificial running under artificial light, awash in the glow of TVs blasting sensational news stories, one more depressing than the next. I felt it was time for a change. Instead, I grabbed the dog leash and headed out for an early morning stroll with a grateful pup.

It was not far into our sojourn when I spied the hummingbird. I have never seen one here in New Jersey and it literally stopped me in my tracks. What a glorious sight to witness that miraculous creature suspended in midair, illuminated by the rays of a beautiful sunrise! It put a smile on my face that lasted the rest of the day.

As I continued my walk, I was remembering the first time I ever saw a hummingbird. I was about 6-years-old, full of life and energy. I loved playing catch with Savage, the neighbor's huge German Shepherd – the dog everyone else was afraid of. I loved exploring the empty lots in the neighborhood and picking wild blackberries for a sweet and juicy summertime snack. And I loved climbing trees. There was an apple tree in our yard next to the empty lot, and one spring day, I had decided to climb up into it to get a closer look at the fragrant blossoms. There, I witnessed my first hummingbird darting among the blossoms, and have been enraptured ever since.

It was brought home to me that life indeed, is one, big, circular experience. What goes around truly comes around: then I was a girl who played with a German Shepherd named Savage, enraptured watching a hummingbird. Now: I'm a grown-up girl walking my German Shepherd, engaged to a man named Savage, enraptured with watching a hummingbird. The simplicity of it is stunning.

What I got out of that morning walk was so much more than a daily dose of exercise. I realized that when I can focus on something, with real awe and gratitude, the rest of life's troubles just melt away. It is impossible to remain anxious when you feel grateful. And nature, for me, provides a healthy antidote to the mountain of worries I can accumulate.

I saw a hummingbird yesterday. You just can't get that feeling from CNN.

I Guess I Needed It After All

I REALLY DIDN'T THINK I needed a vacation. I even tried negotiating my salary higher by attempting to give up my time off from work. It's not that I'm a martyr – far from it! I always have been the type of person to utilize every single day given to me. It was just that I felt my life was working well with the schedule that I had and that between time and money, and not having much of either, vacation didn't seem to be the higher or needed priority.

Boy was I wrong!

I have given workshops on why downtime is needed to recharge internal batteries. So I guess that trying to give up my vacation time was a classic case of "do as I say, not as I do." And also a reminder of just how powerful the mind is in tricking you into believing what you want to believe.

So, since the date of my son's departure for college was looming, and I did have those vacation days, I decided to take a road trip with the two kids who were still here in the States. A trip combining family, friends and new adventure was planned. And the week before vacation? It felt like the LONGEST week of the year! It was at that point that I realized the truth: I really *needed* a vacation!

Now, just back from a wonderful trip, and dreading having to go back to my routine, I am reflecting on the truths I discovered on my journey:

1. **The body doesn't lie**: On day two of the trip I awoke with a horrible sore throat. I figured that it must have been from a combination of singing during the entire 12 hours in the car (thank God for Classic Vinyl on XM radio – and my kids having headphones and their own music!), and talking non-stop with friends and family on my hands-free mobile phone. The reality was

that, as so often happens, I was finally relaxing, which allowed all those latent diseases wrapped up in my tightly-wound, non-vacation state to be released. I ended up visiting an urgent care center and nursed a nasty cold/infection for days. Obviously I needed to relax more than I had thought.

2. **No matter how old you are, people and places can cause emotional time traveling**: Just being around family is enough to evoke old patterns of behavior – often ones that I thought I had moved beyond. It is amazing how deeply we hold feelings from our past! But not all old patterns are bad: I also turned back into a 10-year-old as I galloped and ran down enormous sand dunes, laughing all the way. What a gift to re-experience such a long-forgotten fun memory from childhood!

3. **Validation is welcome at any age**: I had the delight of running into a guy that I knew for a minute in high school. He was the older brother of a friend, and someone who had hung out with the "cool" crowd. When he saw me, he immediately knew who I was *and* was genuinely happy to see me again. The 16-year-old inside of me was doing cartwheels! As much as I marveled at how ridiculous it was to feel that way, I couldn't shake it. Validation matters, no matter how many years it takes to get it!

4. **Things are not always as they appear**: Part three of the trip had been planned so that we arrived at our destination by 10 a.m. Best laid plans... I ended up that day waiting for two hours in the Urgent Care center, with all the

high school students who evidently needed to get their physicals THAT DAY. As I stewed and started to focus on the wasted time, I caught myself and decided to make the best of it. I cleaned out my 800+ e-mails and spent time in semi-quiet meditation. By the time we got to our destination, I realized that those "lost" four hours were truly a blessing, as our destination ended up being a place that we found we did not want to spend a lot of time at anyway. Had I gotten in and out of the clinic, I can only imagine a more unpleasant experience on the other end. You just never know…

5. **The joy in life is in the unexpected**: I had wanted to take my kids to see Sleeping Bear Dunes, a place I fondly remember from my youth. However, the place I remembered and the place we went to were not the same. Evidently what I had thought was Sleeping Bear was not! This was a magnificent location that we explored, making my heart soar. And the best part of the whole trip for me was coming around the corner on the scenic drive, parking the car for one more photo opportunity, and discovering a massive dune that proved to be the PERFECT place to watch an awe-inspiring sunset over a crystal blue, serene Lake Michigan. Truly inspirational.

As I fold the final load of vacation laundry and start the shift back to my work week mentality, I feel truly grateful for my time outside of my routine. Vacation is not a luxury, it's a necessity. And a gift. Glad to be back home again.

I Believe They're Related...

THE OTHER DAY I was putting something down on my dresser and my eye caught the picture of my dad cradling a rather pudgy baby sound asleep in his arms. The very proud grandpa was beaming, holding his first grandchild. Then my eye traveled to the school pictures of my other two children – and I was stopped dead in my tracks. The tilt of their heads, the gentle smiles, the twinkles in their eyes....they are the spitting image of my father! I had never seen this before, but the resemblance was uncanny. My middle son looks exactly like him, but with hair. I know that in his youth, my dad sported an Elvis-like head of hair, so, with that visual in my mind, it was even easier to see the connection.

I was so excited by this revelation that I pulled the pictures off the dresser and went in search of my kids to show them this incredible sight. First, I found my daughter, who said, "Really? You think I look like him?" She agreed, however, that her brother did bear a close resemblance. I shook off her blasé attitude, figuring it's just not cool for a 14-year-old girl to be told she looks like her 84-year-old grandfather. I marched into her brother's room in gleeful anticipation. Once I succeeded in pulling him away from the video war game he was commanding, he glanced over at the pictures and said, "Really? You think I look like him?" Oh come on now – they are practically twins!

Discouraged, I went back to my room to return the pictures and then tried putting a picture of myself next to my dad. Hmmm...just not seeing it. I am sure there are those out there who know my dad and me and would be shocked that I couldn't see the resemblance.

So what is it in us that does not allow us to see ourselves as others do? Like the anorexic who sees herself as fat even though she is skeletal, we have implanted in our brains some sort of image that may not actually jive with reality. Our visions of ourselves are influenced by the opinions of others as well as our own. We literally can convince ourselves that we are not really like the image that appears before us in a mirror.

I know that I have gone through so many physical changes in my life that it is difficult for me to have a clear picture of what I look like. Even more telling are the internal changes and how they affect my vision of myself from moment to moment. I have trouble, at times, believing that anyone thinks that I am attractive and, other times, I feel downright sassy. Add in teenage hormones, and it is no wonder that my kids can't recognize themselves. How they looked in their school pictures just a few months ago is not what they look like now: almost unrecognizable strangers!

Maybe in a few years my kids will be able to look back and see their resemblance to their grandfather. Who knows how long it will take before I do?

I'm a Big Sister and I'm Here to Help

WHEN I WAS IN my early 20s I had a lapel button that said, "My life is a soap opera." It was more of a declarative statement than a conversation starter. I now can see how I used the constant drama in my life as a wonderful distraction from anything that really mattered to me. But, at the time, the drama was both exhilaration and pain on a daily basis, a roller coaster of emotions and intriguing situations. Life these days is pretty mundane compared to then. Thank goodness.

During the moments where I could rise above the insanity and oversee the situation at hand, I would merely shake my head and say, "God must have something really interesting in mind for me to have all these experiences." I figured that there was a reason for each encounter and, if nothing else, they gave me the ability to relate to a lot of people in a lot of different life situations.

I have found that, in many ways, these experiences actually were foretelling my current vocation. My varied and eclectic past has allowed me to be far more empathetic towards others because, in a lot of cases, I've literally "been there, done that." However, I also have another life situation which, when coupled with this empathy, can perhaps come off as not so helpful. Ask my sisters. You see, I'm the oldest. I am a big sister extraordinaire. I believe the word "bossy" has been used to describe me. From my vantage point, my "bossiness" looks like the best of intentions: I have ALL this experience and I am here to help! If someone tells me their tale of woe, not only will I probably have one to match it, but I'll share it with you AND tell you what you should do about it – based on my experience, mind you.

I never really understood how annoying and totally UN-helpful this can be until I saw it reflected in my eldest son's behavior. I believe he has me beat in the bossy category though, as he really doesn't hold back at ALL with his opinions. I, at least, still had that need for everyone to like me so my behavior was tempered a bit. But regardless of the degree of bossiness, I was horrified to witness this mirror being held up to me when I witnessed his behavior with others, particularly his siblings. I believe I started saying "I'm sorry," to my siblings immediately after that and still feel a twinge of guilt whenever we meet.

I continue to believe that the empathy I have for others, as a result of my life experiences, results in a very positive outcome and I work hard to utilize that empathy in ways that benefit others, not myself. At times, I find myself literally biting my tongue to stop myself from chiming in with, "OH I know JUST what you mean because I...." Although come to think of it, just this morning, when a colleague was talking about her kids' sleeping habits, I did have to chime in with how I never had a full night's sleep for 10 years when my kids were small. Well, I guess there's always tomorrow to start again...

Life Is a Giant Thumb

I ONCE HAD A massage from a large, Eastern European woman whose previous occupation, I think, was either a prison guard or Olympic weight lifter. My already tense muscles clenched even tighter at the anticipation of what she was going to do to me. She started by taking her gargantuan thumb, applying it directly on my triple-knotted shoulder muscle, and holding it there...and holding it there...and holding it there. A steady pressure that was unrelenting. I tried to resist it, tried subtly to maneuver myself away, but to no avail. Finally I realized that I had no other choices: my shoulder muscle cried, "Uncle!" and it relaxed.

Life has seemed like a giant thumb to me lately and I have been fighting the pressure every step of the way. As my friend, Mary, noted, "If there was a theme song for your life in the last year it would be, 'What a Long Strange Trip It's Been.'" There are moments when life becomes so ridiculous that I cry a symbolic, "Uncle!" and look around me in amazement. Perhaps that letting go is the lesson for me.

I am lucky to have the time to get away for a few days for a reflective retreat. My saying I am "lucky" is a somewhat new perspective. Up until very recently I have been focusing on what I DON'T have, spending a lot of time in comparisons to what I used to have or could have had. Even this retreat center – I find myself comparing it to another place I've gone in the past and saying things like, "it's not as laid back," "it's more commercialized," "it's more or less than..." Then I feel that thumb coming down and it shocks me back into releasing and seeing where I am, what I am doing and what I have RIGHT NOW.

Right now I'm sitting outside on a hill, overlooking the Berkshire Mountains, which still are cloaked in their early morning fog. The sky is a glorious blue, freshly washed clean from the rumbling thunderstorms of last night. I have the day ahead of me to do with it what I want. My focus is not on "no job," but on "have the gift of time." My life is not "downsized," but "open to possibilities." I am not a "victim of circumstances" but an "adventurer, grateful for the journey."

I was given some sage advice recently: be a leaf, not a salmon. A leaf in the stream goes with flow. It takes advantage of what is being offered to it and experiences all the twists and turns, highs and lows of the journey. The salmon has a mission – to get upstream and spawn. It is focused and goes against the stream – and achieves its goal. And then...it is exhausted and it dies. Both get to the same place, in different ways, with vastly different results. I know my choice.

When I feel that pressure building and the thumbprint of life starts making its slow and steady descent upon me, I choose to release into it, to be open to what else it is that may be ahead for me. It may not be what I had planned, but then again, a "long strange trip" may be just what this adventurer needs.

The Lessons of Lack

I LEFT COLD AND damp New Jersey last week to make my monthly sojourn to the West Coast. I arrived earlier than usual and so took the opportunity to stretch my legs after the long flight and take a relaxing walk. As I stepped out into the sunshine and was greeted by flowers and trees and a glorious blue sky, I felt a rush of gratitude coursing through my body. I realized then, just how long and gray the New Jersey winter had been!

A powerful thought struck me about the wonderful, intense feeling that I had: It was not actually the beauty of my surroundings that was making such an impact on me, but the realization that I had felt a *lack* of that kind of beauty at home.

I remember experiencing that feeling as a child: The anticipation of presents at Christmas or a birthday, something not received at random during the year. The excitement of going out to dinner at a real restaurant – again, a birthday treat. And school shoes! That once a year delight at being able to pick out beautiful penny loafers that would last a whole year.

Once, when I was in my 20s, I felt the excitement of taking my first trip to Paris. I had been teaching for a few years and had saved a whole $300, nothing that ever would have afforded me that opportunity. My college boyfriend, however, was going to be there on business and offered to fly me over, all expenses paid. The excitement of that opportunity was immense. I spent most of my hard-earned savings to get "the perfect dress" to wear, and of course, a matching hat (this was Paris after all!). And while there, he offered to take me shopping and buy me something. I bought a pair of red shoes on the Champs-Élysées...and still have them today! What a thrill that was! Buying shoes today is far more commonplace and just doesn't provide quite the same level of excitement as my purchase in Paris.

Being in "a space of lack" allows me to make room for the joy to follow. Just as I need darkness in order to appreciate the light, there are many opportunities for me to actually be thankful for the lesson that lack provides. Think about these experiences:

- A hug from a long-lost friend or relative
- Holding hands for the first time after a painful breakup
- Spring after a long hard winter
- Saving for, and finally getting, your first house/car/bike, etc.
- Heartfelt birthday wishes letting you know that people are glad you were born
- A real vacation after years of working hard
- A first paycheck
- A piece of chocolate after giving it up for Lent
- Being able to walk on your own after being bedridden

The joy in each of these experiences is amplified because there was a period preceding it in which there was a lack of it. Having a piece of chocolate is always nice, but there is nothing like it when you've been deprived of it for a while. And the simplicity of someone holding your hand when you haven't been touched goes straight to your heart.

The next time I am feeling sorry for myself for not having something, I'll try to shift my perspective and become grateful for the wonderful joy that will follow as a result. If I can learn to do that, there won't be much room left for the negative.

I had originally ended this piece with the glib statement: "So, my only question is this: Will having a lack of cold dreary weather for a time now result in my spontaneous joy when I get back into it, as I return to New Jersey?" Then, amazingly, on my drive home from the airport, breaking through those cold dark clouds into my vision, appeared a glorious rainbow. Seems like I got my answer after all.

Inukshuks to the Rescue!

MY NEW CANADIAN FRIEND, Grace, gave me an inukshuk recently. For you Americans not situated in Governor Palin's neck of the woods, an inukshuk is a statue, or symbol, originating from the Inuit culture and is used as a means to guide or navigate. But for me, even more of the appeal is that it is made out of rock.

I LOVE rocks!

From the rocky shores of Maine, to the secluded beaches in Martha's Vineyard with their sea-smoothed stones, to the beautiful Petoskey stones in Northern Michigan, to an ordinary flat rock suitable for skipping across a pond, I just love them. I've even been known to hug a boulder or two in my day. And when my house sold and the movers carried out the boxes, I'm sure a couple were scratching their heads, wondering what could be so heavy and thinking that it felt like I'd packed a bunch of rocks. I had!

So I was thrilled when my fiancé and I set off on a beautiful fall day to traipse up a mountain trail and take in the glorious fall scenery, only to discover the many rocks along the trail. Nothing is more fun to me than leaping from one boulder to another, trying to figure out which is the steadier path to take.

Have you ever heard the expression, "too much of a good thing"?

As we continued on our trek, which now had shifted from a lovely day outing to a mission to be accomplished, the rocks increased in their numbers and decreased in size, causing one's feet to roll more easily and balance to be lost with greater frequency. I went from adoring these gifts of nature to cursing these worthless nuisances. And they went on and on and on. Now the walk was more of a race just to get to the blasted top so that we could take a break from all these miserable impediments! The way down wasn't any better. For one, we were even more determined to end our travails and just wanted the outing to be over. Forget that romantic notion of a leisurely stroll hand in hand….this was every man for himself (or herself).

And then it happened: They took me down.

I decided that I had two choices: I could lay there and rue the day, and my fiancé's ridiculous idea in the first place, or I could take a breath and enjoy my surroundings. I looked up, realized that it was a beautiful day, and that I was so focused on the negative of the experience that I was totally missing the positive. The leaves were changing, the sky was blue, it was a serene environment, and life – in spite of the rocky road – was good. I'd allowed myself to get caught up in the creeping, pervasive fear that had edged into seemingly every corner of life around me. It's easy to do. It's easy to stumble or fall on the path these days and even those who haven't have seen enough of those who have, and are worried for their own security and safety. I didn't realize that the fear was becoming so ingrained in me until I spent a morning with a group of positive-minded women, who stood out in sharp contrast to the negativity that slowly had been cloaking my psyche.

Sometimes it takes the proverbial fall to make us take notice. It's always our choice, along the way, about how we want to see things. Who knew that those innocuous stones could really prove to be an inukshuk for me? They pointed the way, forcing me to look up. I now can see that, although the way might be rocky, there's always a different perspective that allows you to see the beauty of the situation – even if you look ridiculous in the process.

Life's Highway

I REINVENTED MYSELF WHEN life took a sharp right turn. I thought I was on a nice paved road – despite a few potholes and definite twists and turns. But when I was jettisoned sharply into unfamiliar territory, I realized that I had to change course or be permanently lost.

What do you do when life knocks you for a loop? Illness, death, divorce, loss of a job – all these can take your breath away and make you lose your bearings.

I discovered that, doing things in the same way that I had been, just didn't make sense anymore. I couldn't rely on what I thought I knew. I was broken, but I was broken open, which allowed me to experience new ideas, new thoughts and new ways of being. I've learned that I can try new things and take risks and, although I may be bruised, I will still land on my feet. I can hear that little voice inside, which wisely guides me, and am able, *most* of the time, to actually heed its advice.

The paved road I thought I had been on was merely an illusion. The real gift is being able to truly see where I am going now. I may not know what is beyond the curve up ahead, but I know that my eyes are open and I have all I require to get where I need to go. I'm looking forward to the adventure!

Look Up, Tune In, Turn On

WHEN YOU FIND YOURSELF stuck in a rut, change your perspective. When your life seems dull or overwhelming, look at life from another's viewpoint. A trip to a foreign land will help, as would watching a documentary. Or, how about something closer to home, like having a conversation with your teenager about something you take for granted? I learned this lesson when my son asked me if he could play an album.

My 15-year-old son is into all things 60s and 70s after listening to the soundtrack from the film, *Across the Universe*. It seems that his listening to it had not only sparked his curiosity, but also his visual acuity – he seems to have just noticed the album collection that he has walked past every day of his life. So, last week he asked if maybe I had any music he might like. That's all I needed: I started pulling out albums left and right and lovingly caressing them and reveling in the memories. "Oh, here's Crosby, Stills, Nash & Young – *Déjà Vu* – a classic!" I crooned. "Is that a group?" he countered. **Sigh**. Finally he lit up when I pulled out a Beatles album – a common link. Whoever would have thought that the Beatles would BRIDGE the generation gap?! And then the fun began.

First he put the album on the turntable, put the needle on and told me it didn't work. Lesson number one: turn on the receiver. Next he complained that it kept shutting off. Lesson number two: you place the needle on the OUTSIDE of the record album, not the inside. Getting the needle on the record itself proved challenging, as he kept dropping it just off the edge (with me cringing in the background). Then he had no idea how to find and play the song he wanted to hear. I told him to look at the lines on the record, which seemed to be another foreign concept requiring my intervention once again. "What number is it?" I asked. "Four," came his reply. I placed it perfectly in the groove and the fourth song started… which was not what he wanted. Puzzled, I then asked him, "Well, which side is it on?" Another foreign concept: these things have two sides?! Other lessons included how to remove the record, discussing the fact that if there is one on the turntable already, one must REMOVE that first before putting another on, and then how to handle the record so as not to put fingerprints all over it. And of course, how to put it back in the dust cover.

After all this he just looked at me, put his earphones back in, turned on his iPod and walked away. So much for bridging the gap.

What that interchange with my son did for me though, was to change my thought patterns and jolt me out of my automatic-pilot life. I realized that I take so much for granted and appreciated that blast from the past to remind me that people come from different places, experiences and viewpoints. When I get stuck in a rut, there is another way to look at the situation at hand.

I'm reminded of an image that came to me as I was meditating one day. I envisioned myself high on a precipice. I don't know about you, but the older I get, the less I feel that heights are my friend! So here I was, standing on this mountaintop, staring down at my inevitable demise and feeling a wave of panic engulf me. Not what you would imagine being the side effect of a calming meditation session! But just as I was about to break out in a cold sweat, I heard a steady voice say, "Look up." Slowly I raised my head and looked out instead of down. There, ahead of me, was a gorgeous vista, complete with a sunset over a spectacular mountain range. Immediately the panic evaporated and I was filled with calm and appreciation. Ah – the lesson of perspective: by changing how you look at something, you change how you feel about it.

So even though I may not have converted my son into a Three Dog Night or Seals and Crofts fan, he did give me a chance to look at my life through another's eyes. I can't even imagine the discussion he'll have with his kids that will do the same!

Loving Fish

I'M SITTING IN THE waiting room of the eye doctor, computer on my lap, trying to figure out what wisdom I can impart today. Nothing. Perhaps it's the large diner breakfast that is now making me a little woozy, or the uber-comfy sweater I'm wearing that is keeping me nice and toasty and relaxed on a chilly Saturday. Or maybe my body is just not used to getting more than six hours sleep a night. Thank goodness the World Series is over and I can regain a more "normal" schedule!

I am particularly impressed with the fish tank here and am trying to remember if it always looked like this. These fish are gargantuan! Maybe they need them that big so that the patients who have their eyes dilated can still see them.

There are two carp-like fish (carp on steroids, actually) that bring me back to the days of looking at the fish tank in the pediatrician's office. He had the same kind of fish, but of a more normal size. I remember one day when my son and a little girl were engrossed in watching the fish. The carp/goldfish were drawn to each other and the little girl said, "Look Daddy, the fish are kissing!" It certainly looked like that to me and I pointed that out to my little boy as well. The father then said to his daughter, "No honey, they are not kissing. They are gourami fish and they do that because…" I can't remember exactly what he said but I distinctly remember that let down feeling I got. All the magic of the moment had just been sucked out and replaced by cold, dry facts. I understood the father's need to grasp a teaching moment, but was saddened by it nonetheless. I reassured my son later that, yes, they were kissing…

As I watch these "kissing fish" (as our family chooses to call them) now locking lips (do fish have lips?), I am grateful for both the reminder to keep the magic in my life and the ability to do so. Life is so much more interesting when you can see beyond the facts. And a reminder of affection doesn't hurt either.

Sam I Am

MY FACE HAS CAUGHT up with my hair and I am not happy about it.

Since I was 14-years-old I have had "old hair." In the beginning, my silver streak was a novelty and I loved the way it set me apart. In my 20s it was a way to make me look older than I really was and gave me a certain "credibility" in business environments. Then there were the couple of decades where it mysteriously disappeared...

When I finally allowed my natural silver hues to flow again, my hair color served as a badge of honor and also was very distinctive. I still had a young looking face and the contrast was intriguing. And then, last week, I looked in the mirror...and just saw... old. Old hair, old skin. Ugh. No longer is the "erase minor lines" treatment appropriate – we are *way* beyond the minor lines stage! I have been bemoaning this new phase of my life ever since and, frankly, am feeling quite sorry for myself.

Last night I had the VERY distinct honor of seeing Mr. Sam Moore in concert. Sam "Soul Man" Moore is 75-years young. If you were to pass him on the street, you would think of him as a sweet, slow-moving, old man. But when he opens his mouth and sings, the years just melt away. He is ageless. His voice betrays none of its years and is as crystal clear and soulful as on his recordings from the 60s.

I was in awe of Mr. Moore and his agelessness. It made me realize that when the true spirit of a person is present, there are no boundaries of age or physicality. The true essence of a person transcends this world and invites your spirit to dance.

Perhaps I should just stay away from mirrors and spend more time in front of computer screens, letting my agelessness flow through the words I write. If a man 20 years older than I can transform into a young man by utilizing his gifts, I'm all for it. Sam I Am!

Sweating it Out

IT WAS WHEN I started to think about that Arizona sweat lodge incident that I started to panic. I was sitting in a meeting in the windowless room of an old building. It was a cold morning so the rickety heating system was clanging and clunking away. As the radiator hissed, I took off my coat. Then I removed my scarf. Finally I rolled up my sleeves. I was trying to sit quietly and focus on the topic at hand, but my mind kept going to that horrible sweat lodge catastrophe where three people died from the heat. I checked to make sure that the door was open and reassured myself that I could, indeed, make a break for it, hopefully before I collapsed in a puddle of moisture.

It was about then that a song title from one of my favorite Broadway shows popped in my head: "Always Look on the Bright Side of Life!" How annoyingly happy! Can't they see that I am DYING here?!

I took a minute for a mental body scan and realized that, in fact, only half of my body was melting. The side towards the door and away from the radiator was actually pretty cool. How bizarre. All along I had been totally focused on the negative, when I could have had just as much of a chance of being comfortable. I took a minute to realign my thinking, putting all my energy into existing on that cool side, and eventually the panic subsided and I felt comfortable again.

I remember reading years ago how Shirley MacLaine kept herself warm while in frigid situations by envisioning a furnace inside of her that kept her toasty warm. I have tried to utilize that mind-over-matter principle with varied results but continue to be amazed when it really works. Today was one of those days. It showed me that, not only is my mind very powerful, but that it is very flexible as well. I also learned that I won't be signing up for any sweat lodge experiences anytime soon.

Is It Done Yet?

Fourteen years ago on December 8th I had my house completely decorated, Christmas cards handwritten and mailed, presents bought and probably wrapped – with two boys under the age of 6 at home and a day past my due date for my third child. Today I am lucky to have my house decorated. Cards are a consideration and certainly will NOT be of the mailing variety – e-mail epistles work well for me these days. (Maybe even a blog entry?). I started thinking about presents during a meeting today. Somehow this will all get done....it always does.

I am exhausted thinking about all that I used to do while the kids were little AND I was working full-time. Now my kids are pretty much self-sufficient, I work part-time and yet I can't seem to keep up with the basics. Is it the fact that I am that much older – and have that much less energy? Or have my priorities shifted so that what used to be VERY important is more of a "nice to have/do" now? Probably both.

There are two loads of laundry piled on my bed, last week's newspapers are on the floor, and a bunch of mail is waiting to be sorted through. There is also a soon-to-be-14-year-old who is asking me to snuggle with her now in bed before she falls asleep. Somehow, I think I know where my priorities really lie...

We're Nothing But Ants

I HAVE BECOME REACQUAINTED with the amazing drama that is the life of a teenage girl. No, I am not watching "Teen Moms," on TV, although someone in my house is... The joy of having children is getting to relive your own life all over again. The downside of having children is that you get to live your life all over again. This age 13-18 year-old phase is definitely not one I was looking to repeat!

As I watch the intensity of life through my daughter's eyes, I can't help but be amused at how important she thinks that everything is! And things that are all-consuming today are forgotten tomorrow, only to flare up next week. I am grateful to be "above the fray," having a much different and well-earned perspective on life. It's a lot calmer from where I sit.

This realization made me think that, undoubtedly, the things that I perceive to be earth-shattering today, will someday be looked at with bemusement. Perhaps there is someone/thing already silently smiling with the shake of the head, and seeing the bigger picture. I tend to believe that there is. And this train of thought then takes me to another realization: we humans are really good at complicating a very simple thing. All the wisdom of the ages has told us, as John Lennon put it: All you need is love. Pretty simple concept.

My ex-husband was fond of saying, "We're nothing but ants." I always took that as his glass-half-empty view of life. But I am coming around to seeing some wisdom in it. It's not that we are "<u>nothing</u> but ants," but that, in the grand scheme of things, we merely play a small role. We are just pieces of the puzzle and, although we are important ones, most of the things that we worry about are so very insignificant. Life really is all about the love.

I tried using this mind set yesterday when I found myself getting worked up over some detail that was consuming me. I took a breath and envisioned this higher altitude view of life. Even saying the mantra "we're nothing but ants" helped remind me. And I found, as a result, that the drama and angst just melted away.

I'm going to try explaining this approach to my 15-year-old when she gets home from hanging with her peeps. Somehow, I think that the response I'll get will either involve a bewildered stare or a lot of eye rolling. Such behavior, though, will just bring a smile to my lips (further confusing her), as I send her love and think about how much easier life is on this side of those hormones!

Chapter Six

Balancing it Out

Let Go or Be Dragged

IT WAS AN ORDINARY winter day in Vermont: cold, snowy and no hint of spring in the air. Today I was picking up my car from the repair shop where it had been for the past couple of weeks, being reshaped from a near head-on collision with a drunk driver. His pickup truck had avoided me; the freshly cut logs in its bed had not. Only safety glass and a guardian angel had kept me from losing life and/or limb. A beat-up car I could deal with.

On my way home from the body shop in my newly reconfigured vehicle, I decided to stop and get my mail from the rural route mailbox at the top of my winding drive. Normally, I would pull into the drive (avoiding any cows that might have wandered out of the neighboring yards), walk across the street and pull the contents out of the battered mailbox. But today was cold and I just wanted to get home. So, I did what I had seen so many others do before: pull over to the left-hand side of the road and open the mailbox from my car. I swerved over, proud of my new idea, and went to grab the mail. Drats! Too far away. I'd have to actually open the car door and step out. As I was doing just that, I heard a sound that stopped my heart: an on-coming car. Well, surely he would see me, my headlights beaming in front of him....

I remember seeing the shock on the driver's face as his mind registered what was about to happen. The next thing I knew his car had smashed into mine, my car door had slammed into me, and I grabbed on for dear life. I was being dragged with the car on the icy road. I stayed that way for what seemed like hours until I started to slip downward, scarily close to the tire. I heard a voice say, "Let go."

Really?!

If I let go the car could run over me. Or his car could.

"Let go."

I had no choice, and in a moment of supreme faith and submission, I let go of the car door. I slipped harmlessly under the door as the two cars continued sliding for a few more feet. When I knew that they had stopped, I jumped up and ran to the driver, incredulous about what had just happened. I hadn't even gotten my newly repaired car into my driveway!

The driver, a young kid who probably had just gotten his license, was clearly in shock. He just stared at me. Shortly thereafter, my own shock and adrenaline subsided and I could take in what had just occurred. The ambulance crew that arrived was equally shocked that I was still walking around. Bruised and battered in more ways than one, I was yet awed and grateful, once again, to have avoided a near calamity.

The other day I was in a meeting where I heard someone utter the phrase, "Let go or be dragged." The accident scene came rushing back to me in technicolor. I literally knew the meaning of that phrase. And yet, having been given such a vivid example of the power of faith and surrender, why do I still have such a hard time with the concept and reality of that power? Why do I continue to insist that, "I know what is best," or, "My way or the highway"? Who knows? Is it ego, fear, need for control, or all of the above? Probably all of the above.

All I do know is that I am supremely grateful that, this time, I got my reminder in the form of a simply uttered statement, rather than a full-blown literal example. Maybe I <u>am</u> making progress!

Sybil's Got Nothing on Me

FIRST THERE WAS THE film "The Three Faces of Eve." Next came "Sybil." And now, Steven Spielberg has produced a television show about a woman with multiple personalities called "The United States of Tara." Well, Steven should have just called me because I could have given him a great story line with, "The Two Sides of Janet." My ability to shift personas never ceases to baffle and amaze, at least, me.

A few weeks ago I was basking in the aftermath of a lovely holiday season, filled with opportunities to connect with far-flung loved ones, as well as a lot of down time. I was having a conversation with a friend at 11 a.m., telling her that I couldn't remember the last time that I had I felt so full of joy: a feeling of warmth from head to toe. And I really meant it.

At 11:05 a.m. I received a phone call from a company asking me for payment on an account that I had assumed was closed after struggling with their customer service department months earlier to rectify an annoying situation. Goodbye Joyful Janet – hello Raging Rhonda! In an instant, everything about me changed: my attitude, my intonations, my body language and even my physical appearance as my muscles tensed and face flushed and hands clenched. Thank goodness that this encounter was just over the phone (although I am sure the poor finance department employee still doesn't know what hit him.) It was disturbing to me just how quickly I could shift to such a different perspective.

It has been suggested to me – by many, on many occasions – that perhaps it might be a good idea to consider meditation. A lovely idea. And actually, I've done it before and found it to be a great experience. It's just that, when you are in the agitated mental state where meditation could benefit you the most, engaging in it seems the most improbable solution.

Like exercising: I know I should do it, I've done it before with good results, and yet it is SOOOOOOO hard to get started again!!! Thank goodness for the beginning of a new year to at least have a shot at giving the collective heave ho towards the gym!

So back to this meditation thing...

Whether it be the still-recent good feelings, the now wary looks on the faces of those crossing my path, the increase in "gentle reminders" about meditating, or that I just plain scared myself by my dramatic mood swing, I decided to give it another try. Easing into it, of course, with just 10 minutes a day; not long enough to be considered a true commitment in case it really didn't work out, but long enough in case it did.

And wouldn't you know, it worked.

The most incredible thing I noticed from my brief meditations (besides the immediate lowering of blood pressure) was the realization that there are, indeed, two sides of me – in everyone for that matter. On the one hand, and most obvious to all, is our human side – the one we present to the world, that has our feelings and emotions, hopes and dreams, worries and fears. Most of us live our complete lives in this "outside" reality, as our society and institutions are created from that reality. It's the side of us that asks the question, "What if..."

And yet, there is another side in each us that exists deep within. It doesn't ask the questions – it has the answers. Its motto is, "All is well," because it really is. The image that came to my mind is this: Our "worldly self" is this hard outside shell (our physical selves) and our inner self is this fluid, formless entity that has no beginning and no end. There is no worry "inside," because there are no boundaries to worry about. The most "real" example of this entity to me was on Inauguration Day in 2009: billions of people around the world shared this universal feeling of hope and even joy. It was not about the man we had elected, but what he represented – it was that internal energy, that "all is well" knowing. Whether you were in Washington, DC, Kenya, Hawaii or in front of your TV in New Jersey, you felt a part of that amazing energy. There were no arrests in DC that day in spite of millions of people in the city. I don't know about you, but I have to believe that the absence of violence was tied into something greater.

Learning to tap into that calm knowing is part of my ongoing process and experience. It began for me with the willingness to even *consider* the possibility of its existence. Giving consideration to the idea that "we are spiritual beings having a human experience" also gave me pause and opened that door of possibility a little wider. And finding an activity, whether it be walking the dog, taking a hike or sitting quietly for even 10 minutes a day, that allowed me to quiet my mind and tap into that beautiful place sealed the deal.

Lest you think that I have completely changed my ways and am contemplating joining a group of monks in Bhutan (although, hmmm, that doesn't sound so bad…), I'm still the magical combination of Joyful Janet and Raging Rhonda, with, probably, a couple more personalities sprinkled in for good measure. What I have learned is that regardless of what face I am wearing today, inside, I am always the same person. And when I succumb to the ambient fear that is threatening to engulf us, I just need to dive back down inside and remember that great truth: that in spite of what things seems to be on the outside, all IS well.

A Decision of the Heart

I'VE BEEN LIVING IN my head for the past few weeks and believe me, it ain't a pretty place! It is amazing how the gift of imagination can flip and become a harbinger of fear and doubt. Sadly, I have many bedfellows in this doom and gloom mentality, and the outlook doesn't seem to be getting all that much rosier. I have been feeling overwhelmed, overextended and overburdened with life and knew that I needed to do something. So I got a puppy.

Perhaps there are those of you out there who are aghast at what I just said. Well, I just got ONE puppy, not eight. I don't think that I have gone that far over the edge (yet). And believe me, there are moments when I do doubt my own ability to reason. But, in some ways, it was the sanest decision I've made in a long time.

A large part of my life lately has been spent trying to "figure things out." I have been consumed with numbers and scenarios and what-if schemes. I have spent hours planning and replanning. I track time, expenses, what I eat, and what needs to be done. Frankly, I am exhausted. So, as part of my grand plan, and true to form, I decided that it was time to start to THINK about what type of dog to get IN THE FUTURE to fill the void left by our beloved Bernese Mountain Dog, Tessie, who recently had passed away. The plan was to take the kids down to look – just LOOK – at the puppies where my fiancé's daughter works. (Besides, then I could check off the "to do" of having the kids meet each other).

Best of intentions: I had thought I had planned everything, told them countless times we were JUST LOOKING, and brought nothing with me that would allow me to actually buy a dog. I just didn't plan on allowing my heart to play any role in this outing. Obviously someone in a bigger place had plans other than mine!

One look, one babysoft cuddle, one puppy kiss, and my heart took over, pushing my previously dominant, logical mind far into the background. Here was what was missing for me – allowing myself that gift of unconditional love. The "I don't care where you are, who you are, or where you are going" kind of in-the-moment love, free of human trappings and failings. I was hooked. The kids' pleading not to go home "empty lapped" was nothing compared to the insistent voice of my heart. And so, Miss Lily has entered our lives and changed them forever.

I am someone who is blessed with a loving family, amazing friends, wonderful business associates and a truly adoring partner. The love that surrounds and envelopes me is not lost on me nor taken for granted. But at times, and unfortunately all too frequently of late, I can find myself slipping into that old pattern of living in the future and forgetting what is happening right now. There is nothing like the insistent love of a pet to bring you back to the moment and remind you of what is really important.

Life can be filled with slips and slides, mountains to climb and obstacles to overcome. We can make plans, chart courses of action and align resources to achieve our goals. But when all is said and done and planned and executed, nothing compares to the purity and completeness of a decision of the heart.

Keep Hope Alive

IT'S A FUNNY THING, this "hope" thing. It's at times elusive and yet, in reality, I think, it is something that is always camped outside the door like an anxious pet eager to be let in.

There are times when I listen to inspiring stories and feel as though I am an observer in an ivory tower, sipping tea and looking down upon the huddled masses. My eyes tear up appropriately and I say a, "Good for them!" Never once will those kinds of tales offering glimmers of hope pierce my well-honed emotional armor.

Other times I will hear those tales and it will be as though the person is speaking in tongues. "My life was miserable and just when I thought there was no hope, blah, blah, blah, blah, blah...." I just don't get what they are saying. Or maybe, I simply don't believe them.

But there are other days, like today. Today, while I wasn't overjoyed or optimistic or wildly energetic, I did feel <u>willing</u> to believe. And, just allowing that ever-so-slight opening, allowed hope to rush on in. It's an amazing phenomenon – kind of like how mosquitoes can get through screen doors. And, once in, hope has a tendency to take over. It changes the "nevers" to "maybes" and the "impossibles" to "why nots." It lightens and brightens us from the inside out.

I got a fortune cookie tonight with dinner that said, "You are free to invent your life." As I sat there and pondered the myriad of possibilities of that statement, my daughter said, "You must really like that one – you're really thinking about it." I did. I was grateful to have just enough hope to believe that my "fortune" was true.

Janet M. Neal

Life Lessons in Triplicate

IT BEGAN INNOCENTLY ENOUGH *with the receipt of a beautiful e-mail message that spoke gently of the power inherent in letting go. How lovely, I thought – and then saved it because you just never know when that kind of message might be of value to someone I know. The "powers that be" must have split a gut laughing over that one! I get my life lessons presented to me not once, or even twice, but generally three times. I think that a good part of the reason why I need a triple dose of wisdom is that because I am so busy, I tend to ignore the first, take a slight interest in the second, and have no choice but to deal with the third. This time I must REALLY have been out of control because normally, any one of the lessons would have been an attention-grabber. Evidently I needed all three this time to really do the trick. I believe that getting that e-mail was no coincidence. My lesson at hand is learning, again, to let go.*

I wrote those words after delivering my eldest to his dorm to begin his college career. Now, this is the child who, since maybe day two of his life, has been a totally independent spirit. He went off to summer camp at age 12 for a month in the wilderness with no communication home. He's traveled internationally by himself. He spent the last two years of high school 3000 miles away at a boarding school. So, when the boxes were moved and suitcases unpacked and it finally was time for the goodbyes, I was shocked when the tears welled up in my eyes. OK, they spilled over for a time as well. After all the goodbyes we've said, this one was different. It was saying goodbye to my little boy and watching him walk away as a young man. I'm getting all teary now just thinking about it. Letting go of him, allowing him to transition to this next, exciting stage of his life was scary and yet, reaffirming. Life is a series of transitions, and to hold oneself or others back is to deny the full array that life has to give. Just imagine the experiences that he had as he stepped into this new space. Actually, I'll allow you to do that…there are some things a mother just shouldn't imagine! So, that goodbye should have been enough, right?

Nah. Next on my plate was to say goodbye to my staff as I began to shut down my business, The Professional Women's Center (PWC). Life, the economy, an idea ahead of its time… whatever the reasons, the result was the same: I had to shut the doors. This decision to let go was fraught with copious amounts of anxiety, hours of soul-searching and numerous attempts at self-deception. Ultimately, it was when I was able to truly release any ego woven into a possible outcome that I was able to secure my answer and, thankfully, serenity about the decision. The lesson really had come full circle: I let go, just as I had done when I started the process to launch the PWC, and things were able to flow and life got a whole lot easier. Getting out of my way seems to be a big lesson in letting go for me.

And lastly, just to complete the trifecta, I put my home of 15 years on the market. This is the house I'd said I would never leave, merely because I have too much junk to move. I have learned that there was absolute truth in that tongue-in-cheek statement. Again, I thought I was good with this decision – until I had to start getting rid of old toys and mementos from the "good old days." I've realized how much of my life was woven into the fabric of that dwelling, not to mention the fact that it's the only home that two of my three kids have ever known. To learn that our "home" is really wherever we go, that things are merely reminders of memories but the memories are always within, and that we don't need so much STUFF to be happy…these are lessons that are only beginning to be experienced and appreciated.

Letting go of one thing/thought/belief seems to start the unraveling of so many more. And each knot that is loosened brings a little more breathing room and the space to grow in new and unknown directions. I guess that I'm grateful to be so pig-headed that I needed all this evidence to get the message. I certainly would not have had this fire-hose of emotion if I'd only listened just to that e-mail. I'm actually excited now, for the first time in a long time, about what might lie around the corner. I've come to realize that you can't embrace what life has to give you if you're clinging to the past. I'm ready to go forward into life with open arms, an open heart…and a much cleaner house!

Never Say Never Again

I EXPERIENCED ANOTHER "NEVER say never" moment this week. Up until then, if you had told me that I would willingly get up at 2:30 a.m. to drive to see the sunrise – on vacation – my reply would have included, among other things, the word "NEVER!" But I have learned that the Universe does not hear the word "never," so, there I was. Just like when I told my mother upon graduating from college that I would NEVER live in New Jersey. I now have been here for more than 20 years. You'd think that I would have learned…

Anyway, I was on vacation in Arizona, yet another "never" experience: "I will never go to Arizona in July!" There was no question that I needed a vacation and my idea of one was a beach, cool breezes, and lots of dozing off. So, here I was, going to the Grand Canyon to experience the sunrise. And yes, although 2:30 in the morning is an unfathomable time to travel anywhere, the trip was worth it. Just my fiancé and I ….and a busload of Japanese tourists. Oh well, at least the ride didn't involve my needing to think about anything. I was just beginning to revel in the semi-solitude, and the gradual unveiling of the magnificence before me, when the sun finally popped, greeted by a serenity-shattering "AHHHH!" enthusiastic clapping, and other gleeful expressions by the gang, appropriately, from the Land of the Rising Sun. To which I became annoyed. How "touristy", I thought with annoyance. But then, gratefully, just a moment later, I saw their reactions from a different perspective. How perfectly lovely to show such childlike wonder and appreciation for something that is truly miraculous and awesome. I realized that I loved their spontaneity and decided to adopt an attitude of inquisitiveness and gratitude for the remainder of the trip.

Being in awesome, natural surroundings afforded me many opportunities to practice my new attitude. I'd heard that Sedona was a spiritual place, so I decided to "act as if," pretending that I was receiving messages in everything I saw. I figured that even if it weren't because of the "vortex" or the energy or the whatever, thoughts that were somewhere in my conscious or unconscious mind were coming forward for a reason and probably would be worth looking at.

We did many hikes up and down red rocks and deep caverns. On one trail, I found a blue rock that was shaped exactly like a human ear. I decided to take this as a sign that I needed to listen more. Three times we came across cacti in the shape of a heart. I took this to mean that love can appear to be painful, but at its core, is soft and mushy and life-sustaining in difficult times. There were ravens or crows everywhere. One was even in the parking lot walking next to me. That bird just plain spooked me. But I also watched two of them in a tree: one was squawking away and the other just sat there, as if it patiently was waiting for its partner to finish its ranting. Then, when the squawking seemed to be done, they flew off together. I took that as a message that sometimes you just need to let your partner vent before you can move on together. I was serenaded by cicadas. At least I think that's what they were: I heard them but never saw them. It was a reminder that just because you can't see something, it doesn't mean it's not real. And lastly, the mountains themselves were very inspirational. So stately, powerful, elegant and unique – no two were the same. Weathering the good and the bad, they were magnificent in the strength that they portrayed. They offered a big lesson on the power of *being* rather than *doing*.

Every bit of nature I encountered had some sort of message for me. But the biggest one may have come from someplace closer to home: listening to myself. Our last hike was a beauty – traversing gradually up the side of Doe Mountain. About two thirds of the way up, my fiancé, who is, shall we say, less than excited about heights, decided that he had gone about as far as he wanted to go. Normally, I would agree with him and go back down. But, that day, I felt that I needed to reach the top. So on I went, alone. It was such an invigorating feeling to be alone on that mountain, watching my perspective change with each step. But, as I neared the top and could finally see the summit, I began to feel sick. I found myself listening to some old thought patterns: telling myself that this was good enough, look how far you've come, what a great view from here, and who would know the difference anyway? I would know the difference I realized, so I pushed on.

I cannot tell you what a rush it was to reach the top. Being a part of that 360-degree vista was amazing. But, even more so, was the knowledge that I had pushed myself past the point that, in the past, would have held me back, and I came out on the other side better for it. As I walked back down the narrow trail I practically felt like skipping. A few loose rocks quickly brought me back to reality on that one! As I was thinking about how much fun this adventure had been, I flashed back to being 10-years-old and exploring the fields and woods in my neighborhood. I had experienced the same feelings: freedom, exhilaration, confidence, curiosity and gratitude for each newly discovered treasure. I felt so connected with that younger me and realized that, at that moment, I had never felt so totally "me." It brought me to tears. As I stood on that mountain path, engulfed in gratitude, a huge Yellowtail butterfly, which had followed me all the way up the mountain, circled me and flew off. My lesson for that moment was complete.

There are probably other experiences awaiting me in my life that will give me a chance to push myself and come out stronger on the other end. No doubt there will be challenges with my career, my family, my relationships or even in dealing with myself. But I know that I have the tools and the capacity to deal with them. I came back from this vacation feeling as if I had escaped the confines of my mind. The trip had been energizing and expanding and gave me the impetus to keep going. My sister ran her first marathon last year at 48-years-old and she told me that the run was a similar experience to mine. I'll trust her on that one because….well, I'd say, "I'll never do that"….but we know where that could lead!

Singing Loud for All to Hear

I DID MY PART to spread some Christmas cheer yesterday: I sang loud for all to hear. And I watched the movie "Elf" (for the fourth time) with my daughter. (For those not familiar with the movie, it's cute and my first line, above, is a quote from it....)

But getting back to my singing....I did it! I followed through with my commitment to sing a cantata with my church choir, even though at times my ability to do so was questionable. It was truly a humbling experience for me. I had always thought that I had a decent voice, although not a consistent one. Being surrounded by experienced singers, even some professional ones, REALLY highlighted just how inconsistent I am! If I hit one note in three measures, it was a good session! And let's not even go there regarding the words. They were all in Latin, something I managed to never study. The director kept scolding us for using diphthongs. I didn't even know what that meant...

Saturday we had a dress rehearsal with the orchestra—a lovely, seven-piece string group. I knew that I really was in trouble when I realized due to my height, that I would have to stand in the first row. I had thought that, maybe, I could hide behind the real singers and get away with my less-than-stellar performance. Now, not only would everyone in the congregation see me, but the director REALLY could give me the evil eye. I felt as if I were trying every ounce of his patience and good Christian values. I was attempting not to take it personally when he announced that he was quitting after only being there for four months. Seriously.

The other thing besides my singing ability that I was worried about was my facial expressions. I realized that, all during rehearsal, I had been rolling my eyes or grimacing every time I did something wrong. In other words, frequently.

Probably not a good thing for someone in the front row of the choir to be doing. I was glad that we had a dress rehearsal so that, along with my singing, I also could practice being facially neutral... It wasn't easy.

Sunday came and I was a bit nervous. It did help that the minister told me that I looked good in my choir robe. Well, the purple stole did work well with my hair color. I could only hope that others would focus on that rather than actually look at my face. I wore my new contacts to look especially stunning – and then realized that I had not brought my reading glasses to the church and could not actually see the words of the song. Great. And to make matters worse, it was a packed house. Who knew that many so people would come to church? What happened to the days of empty pews? Didn't these people have more important things to do, like sleeping or shopping or getting ready to watch a football game?

What helped me in the end was realizing that this performance really was NOT about me. It was being given in a gorgeous church, beautifully decorated for Christmas, and lovely music was to be performed by an amateur choir accompanied by professional musicians. I decided that this would be as close to Broadway as I was going to get, so why not make the best of it and "fake it till you make it." I decided to pretend that I was as good a singer as the professional soloist next to me and, if nothing else, I looked good in the robe!

So, even though I could not see the words, or pronounce them correctly, or even hit every note, I sang my heart out. Only once did I jump back into my head and start to panic, but I was able to recover quickly. The words of a very sweet choir member kept ringing in my head: "It's not about the individual voice, but how you can blend with the others to make it bigger and better." I thought that I could do that. And the result was that the blending of the voices was beautiful and uplifting and I didn't grimace once, at least not that I knew of.

They asked me to sing on Christmas Eve as well. Well, hey, you never know...

Getting the Right Fit

MY SON SHOWED ME his red, blistered feet the other day and sure enough, he had what I call, "New York feet." They come from walking blocks and blocks in fashionable, but not necessarily comfortable shoes, in ungodly hot weather in the city. I figured that only women suffered from this condition, but it makes sense that he would as well, since he is the same kid who, as a toddler, had such fat little feet that the kindly old shoe salesman actually had to work hard to try to find something to fit him.

I was thinking about how many times I have tried to make my life fit into an attractive package so that it looked good on the outside but, in truth, I was very uncomfortable inside. Actually, more times than I'd like to count. I would come home with "New York feet of the Soul," in emotional pain and miserable and swearing I would never behave to impress again. And then, a few days later, I'd be right back at it because, as Fernando (aka Billy Crystal) would say "It's not how you feel, it's HOW YOU LOOK!" I would suffer with the wrong fit in relationships, jobs, friendships, living arrangements – anything, as long as I felt that the situation at least made me look "mahvelous."

And then, interestingly, one day I found myself in a situation that fit well, and boy, what a difference!! If you only have worn shoes that are too small and then one day put on a pair that really fits you will know what I am talking about. It is like night and day. Having something that fits well changes your whole attitude! You are no longer in pain – physical, psychic, emotional or mental. You are free of constraints and open to possibilities. You are not living in fear of the next step and what it may bring. Living with a good fit truly opens up your world.

I finally am learning to notice when something is not fitting me well. I have that first step down pretty well. I'm now working on learning to do something about a "bad fit" before the pain becomes unbearable. The time frame between noticing it, and actually doing something about it, is shortening, but there is a lot of room for improvement.

Life is meant to be worn like a loose garment. I'm getting more and more comfortable with that style every day.

Relationship Hoarders

Social networking is nirvana to relationship hoarders. I know – I'm one of them. I've come to this realization by observing just how excited I get whenever someone from my past reaches out to me. I believe the proper term would be "giddy."

Many years ago, I heard the story of The Prodigal Son and just did not understand why this bad boy got so much attention. Now, I totally get that "killing the fatted calf and throwing the party" thing. Obviously, this father was also a relationship hoarder. Having someone from the past make contact is like having a part of yourself return. And it also is a great excuse for a party.

I recognize that there are two types of individuals: those who love to keep ties to the past and those who believe that the past is the past and let's just keep it at that, thank you very much. Even in my own family we vary wildly. My mother stated to me, "Why in the world would you want to get back in touch with those people?" This question is coming from a woman who still has lunch with elementary school friends, mind you, so I don't necessarily think that she'd balk if someone got back in touch with her either. I think that past connections just don't feel, to her, like finding missing jigsaw puzzle pieces. My ex, on the other hand, had a hard time coming up with people, outside our current circle of friends, to invite to our wedding. He was disdainful about getting back in touch with even close friends from the past. Doing so was as foreign a concept for him as NOT getting in touch with them would be for me.

I've always been like this about the past. Way before there were computers, when we actually wrote letters, I was notorious for sending birthday cards to everyone – even people I barely knew. I wrote lengthy letters to friends I'd met the week before – and continued to do so for extended periods of time. I distinctly remember getting back in touch with a good friend after not communicating for 20 years, and the feeling, similar to that of finding a lost part of me, was overwhelming. If there were fatted calves in the area, they would have been in serious danger of losing their lives!

I love the concept that I am tied by this invisible, virtual cord with people whom I've known and who have known me. Perhaps it's a security blanket of sorts so that I know that I actually did have a past, even if my less-than-stellar memory can't always put all of the past's pieces together. Maybe it's the old "Sally Field syndrome": "You like me! You really, really like me." Perhaps most of all, I just love seeing pieces of this quilt of my life being woven together in front of me. For example, thanks to social media, I know that one of my third grade students from Michigan knows one of my corporate bosses from Vermont and they now both live in Texas. I can't help but think there are more connections out there that are, as yet, undetected, just waiting to be uncovered.

On those days when life becomes overwhelming and I feel like such an insignificant cog in a massive wheel, I only have to look at these amazing connections and see the warm and wonderful creation they have woven that makes the world a smaller, cozier place to be. I can't wait to greet the next "old" friend virtually, or uncover another amazing mutual connection. Bring on them calves!

Shine On!

SOMETIMES I'M AFRAID THAT I've spent so much of my life hiding my light that I have become too comfortable with the darkness. I think, for some of you, this statement might be a bit of a shock. I work hard to make sure that I project a positive image, and, by nature, I am an optimist. I also have built a business on motivating others. So why would I ever say that I am comfortable with the darkness?

The truth lies in the words, "I work hard." Some days the minutia in my mind becomes overwhelming. Gray, leafless days that stretch on and on tend to numb my spirit. Crawling under the covers or into a hole sound awfully appealing. But I have been given the gift of being reminded by those around me that I have a choice about which thought pattern I wish to follow at any particular moment. Some days I want to choose the "easier" path of non-caring or frustration and I allow myself to start wallowing in the depths of self-pity. And then, someone, or something, comes along to shine a light on me and illuminate the reality of my situation.

Take yesterday, for instance. I had had "one of those days." Trying to get a car registered, I left home early and then got lost in a not-too-savory area looking for the DMV. Once I finally got there, the line to get IN the door was down the block. Great way to start the day. I decided to give up, try later and just go to work early or at least on time for once, only to find myself behind every school bus and construction vehicle in New Jersey. Frustration was now piling on top of frustration. Later, I decided to try another DMV location, thinking that it MUST be better than the other one, only to find the same scenario and I ended up standing in line for two hours. I couldn't even come home to blog about it because my website had been down for a week, leaving me "speechless." Finally, I decided to vent on Facebook, hoping to get a little sympathy from my friends. Instead, I got a note from someone in the South who had been hit by that week's horrific, disabling storms. Talk about snapping me back into perspective!

The other side of this attitude coin has to do with allowing myself to be "big." I know that, as a child, it was very important to me to fit in. In order to do that, I needed to "tone it down," making my personality/talents/opinions more mainstream and less open to criticism. Years of this conditioning created a neural pathway which became the "go to" response when faced with any opportunity to shine. Learning to accept myself, embracing my gifts, and allowing them to shine has been hard work for me. It still can be.

Spiritual activist, author and lecturer, Marianne Williamson said it best, in a quote that resonates to my core:

> *Our deepest fear is not that we are inadequate.*
> *Our deepest fear is that we are powerful beyond*
> *measure.*
> *It is our light, not our darkness, that most frightens us.*
> *We ask ourselves, Who am I to be brilliant,*
> *gorgeous, handsome, talented and fabulous?*
> *Actually, who are you not to be?*
> *You are a child of God.*
> *Your playing small does not serve the world.*
> *There is nothing enlightened about shrinking*
> *so that other people won't feel insecure around you.*
> *We are all meant to shine, as children do.*
> *We were born to make manifest the glory of God within*
> *us.*
> *It is not just in some; it is in everyone.*
> *And, as we let our own light shine, we consciously give*
> *other people permission to do the same.*
> *As we are liberated from our fear,*
> *our presence automatically liberates others.*

For today, I choose to shine. May your path be equally as bright.

Tapping into My Inner Martian

JOHN GRAY'S 1992 BEST seller, "Men are From Mars, Women are From Venus," gives suggestions for improving couples' relationships by understanding their styles of communications and their emotional needs. I read the book and was slightly horrified to find that I really identified in most cases with the male profile. This is one of those deep dark secrets that, up until now, I have not shared with anyone. While I'm on a roll, I'll confess that I also do not stop to ask for directions.

I identified most with the book's statement that men need to enter "the cave" before talking with their wives or significant others following a day at the office. But my contention is that there are a LOT of women out there that would LOVE to enter "the cave" and get a little quiet time before greeting a partner or family, but, somehow, it just doesn't work out that way. How many mothers of curious toddlers would love just to be able to go to the bathroom without being followed EVERYWHERE? Some days, even my adoring dogs' exuberant greeting at the door is just too much. A little peace and quiet upon arriving home from work would be just the ticket.

In many ways, I think that men, instinctively, get the concept of "balance" better than women do. Or, perhaps women get it instinctively, but allow their emotions and guilt to override their understanding of balance. It use to drive me crazy when my ex-husband could lounge around on Sundays, seemingly guilt-free, while I was running around taking care of this thing and that. Learning to give myself permission to relax and unwind after a busy week like he did meant letting go of expectations and resentments that were, pretty much, all self-created.

I was talking today with a friend whose husband is on an extended work commitment that takes him away from home for many months. Her comment to me, when I asked how that situation is for her, was, "I'm looking forward to reading a book!" I totally related and wondered to myself why it is that we women can't carve out that time for themselves. We'll make the time to do the household chores, to put someone else's needs before ours and to attend to the feelings of family and friends but, somehow, shuffle our own needs to the bottom of the "To Do" list.

My kids are older now and pretty much live in their rooms when not hanging with their friends. So getting some quiet time alone is not nearly as difficult as it used to be. But every once in a while, I still need to announce to any interested parties within earshot that I am taking a timeout and I close myself in my room for a little bit. These few moments of rest give me such renewed energy and the ability to handle the inevitable, daily stress.

It is amazing what you can learn when you are open to getting the message ....even if that message is coming from Mars.

Janet M. Neal

Winter's Weeding

THERE IS SOMETHING SO very rewarding about shoveling snow. It's the winter equivalent of weeding a garden. When I first look at the task at hand, I shudder and think of a million other things I just HAVE to do now, or whom I could get to do it for me. But once I resign myself to the task and get into the mindless rhythm of it, I find myself smiling. I love the way my muscles respond to the challenge, even though I know that, while I couldn't tell you which ones I'm using in the moment, I will be made painfully aware of their presence in the morning! I love the relative silence that envelopes the otherwise bustling block. Gleeful squeals from kids on sleds, or playful barks of dogs, overjoyed with their snowy wonderland, replace the loud sounds of cars rushing by. The scraping of the shovel against sidewalk is like striking gold, and each exposed patch of the concrete path makes me swell with pride at my accomplishment.

Shoveling, like any mindless chore, gives me a great opportunity to give my conscious mind a job to do and frees my unconscious mind to roam freely. Ideas come spilling forth and the excitement of a job well done combines with the excitement of new things to do or write or imagine. Before I realize it I am nearly done and return all my focus to "breaking through" to the other side and completing my mission.

I walk back inside, feeling tired but proud. I go to the picture window to survey my handiwork, just as the plows storm by and refill the bottom of the driveway. The sidewalk, bare a minute ago, already is being covered by the still-falling snow. I sigh, and then smile, remembering the sweet time of escape that I just experienced. Looks like Mother Nature is going to give me lots of opportunities to experience it again!

Embracing Silence

FM RADIO IN OUR family car saved me from having to hear the lyrics, "Roll out those lazy, hazy, crazy days of summer!!" yet again. Don't get me wrong – I love Nat King Cole's music. But really...AM radio?? In today's vernacular, it is *so* lame. It's about the same way my kids feel when they grab the cord to plug in their iPods to rescue themselves from having to listen to all those songs that I like – which are pretty much the same ones I was listening to back then when I escaped from AM radio! But, in reality, my favorite thing to listen to these days in my car is silence. I get in, turn off the radio, and revel in the quiet.

This morning I was in an hour-long meeting where no one spoke for more than half of it. OK, part of the meeting was devoted to meditation. But then, the silence continued. Usually, after a couple of minutes of silence, I start to feel uncomfortable, needing to fill the space. Today, I was surprised at how much I enjoyed just *being*. I realized that my life has slowed down in the past few weeks and how comfortable I have become with the concept of being, not doing. I can feel my blood pressure lowering, my positive attitude returning and my overall state of well-being vastly improving.

As I look at the clock now, and realize that I have to leave for work, I am grateful for not feeling rushed or overburdened. And you can bet I won't be turning on the radio when I get in the car.

From the Mouths of Babes

"When the student is ready, the teacher will appear"
  – Buddhist Proverb

My "teacher" arrived more than 20 years ago. My eldest son came into this world full of passion and energy. An intense baby, I knew he would turn into a remarkable adult – if we both survived his childhood! And so far, my prediction looks to be right on track.

This child brought intensity and passion into my life at a time when I was insulated and numb. I had lost connection with many of my inner feelings and was alienated from any direction in my life. And here was a child who was so clear, so passionate, so intense – I could only look on in amazement. At age 12 he decided to try ski racing, like his older cousins, and did the local ski resort timed runs when we were there. The next year he decided that he wanted to join the development team. He made a goal of not only doing those runs, but of doing them well enough to qualify to go to the national time trials. And he accomplished those goals. The following year he joined the ski team and made a goal of qualifying for the Pennsylvania state finals, even though it was his first year of competition and he was far behind the pack. And he did it. He went on to qualify for other races and then the Junior Olympics, always setting a goal and, because of having a singular focus, achieving it.

At some point I stopped just watching in amazement and realized that this child was indeed in my life for a reason. Among the many other things that he has taught me, is that he is a master teacher about following your passion. He always has been one to listen to his heart and to do what he feels needs to be done. During his freshman year of college he set aside competitive ski racing in order to start a fraternity

AND a business. The following year, he went back to the skiing (in addition to the other activities!) and told me that he realized just how much he had missed it and how alive he feels when he is on the slopes. Once again, he had tapped into his passion and it had refueled him, giving him what he needed to keep going despite that crazy, college-life schedule he kept.

I don't think that I'll ever feel things as passionately as he does – I don't think that many people do! But I have learned from him that it is not only OK to follow your heart, but necessary to do so. It is what keeps us going, what gives us the energy to do what needs to be done. It's what makes it all worthwhile.

May you find your passion – and live it!

Getting the Lesson

Life is a series of stepping stones, taking me on an interesting and unpredictable journey. Well, that's how I look at it when I am in a good space. When my world is a little darker, it seems as if I've strayed off a path and found myself hopelessly lost in the woods. Today I'm able to see how, once again, I've been given even more life experiences from which I can pull in order to empathize with others. The latest experience is the feeling of not having any clue which way to turn or where I want to go – and how to get out of this rut.

I've worked with several clients over the years who were just stuck. They know that they don't like where they are, but don't know how to change and/or where to go. I always have felt that I understood their dilemmas but really, if I have to be honest, I was always that person who knew what she wanted to do, and did it, since I was a little kid. So, evidently, the Universe felt that it might be good for me to experience this feeling of limbo first-hand! I'm here to say, it ain't a pretty feeling!

I believe that thoughts influence actions, so I knew that the first place to start was with my thoughts. But what was I to think if I had no idea what I wanted or where I should go? A very frustrating situation! I realized that I had to step back even further from my usual "figure it out" mode, and learn to be content with the mantra, "I am open to opportunities that come in my path." And I found that the key word was "open." After a period of time of negative thoughts and energy, I had found myself closing down in a protective manner. So, just being willing to be open was a big first step for me.

One day, as usual, deep in my thoughts and trying to figure out my life, I run into a woman whom I've known for years and we have a pleasant conversation about her business.

She tells me about how great things are going and how she's thinking of expanding the product line. How exciting for her, I think, wishing that I could be in her shoes and be excited about something. She goes on to tell me that she is thinking of adding a business development person to her office staff with this new area of her business and if I knew of anyone, to let her know. Of course, I answer in the affirmative, always willing to be of service. When she leaves, I immediately go into processing mode, trying to figure out who would be good for her. And then, somewhere deep inside of me, comes a little voice saying, "What about you?" The question startled me, and stopped me from my ruminations. What about me? Could this be an opportunity for ME? I remembered the "be open" mantra I had been putting out there daily and, if nothing else, I knew that I owed it to myself to check out this potential opportunity.

Long story short: I got that job and it feels SO right! I am working with a wonderful group of people in a wonderful environment and I am thrilled!

Nice when the teacher gets the lesson...

Losing My Hearing

I CONSIDER MYSELF TO be a fairly secure person. I've spent a lot of time working on discovering who I am, what I value, and what I want out of life. So, it surprised me the other day when I found myself slipping into old patterns of self-doubt. It seemed that I had lost the ability to hear myself.

I was waiting to meet a potential new business associate, a relationship I was anticipating becoming both lucrative and mutually beneficial. As I sat there, I felt the old butterflies starting up, the palms beginning to sweat. My thoughts shifted to what the man I was meeting may ask me, what I could say and how could I impress him. It was at that point that, fortunately, my "hearing" returned.

As children, our internal hearing is acute. Our points of reference are internal and our reactions and actions are based on what we "hear" inside. As we mature, our orientation starts to shift as we become aware of those around us. Our teen years are the most confusing, in part because of the contradiction in what we are hearing. Our inside voice is screaming at us, yet we are acutely aware of those around us and the need to assimilate. It is soon after this point that we make the unconscious decision as to which voice we are going to heed.

For many years the voices outside of myself became the dominate ones. My internal voice, once booming, had become a whisper. Sometimes it was silent. It was at this point – when I started to value the outside much more than that inside voice – that I found myself out of balance. How *could* I be content, when there was such an important part of me being stifled?

To find that balance, I needed to rediscover my inner voice. The key was to listen. It was there. It was just being suppressed. Getting quiet is one great way to accomplish that reconnection. I just need to stop what I'm doing and take 10 minutes a day just to sit and listen to how I feel, ask myself questions and wait for the reply. Or I write about a topic and keep writing until the truth starts to pour out. I once heard a sermon at Christmas where the minister spoke of the shepherds who were the first to receive the message of the baby's birth. She pointed out that others may have been given the message as well, but the shepherds were the only ones quiet enough to hear it.

As I sat waiting for my meeting to begin, I regained my hearing. I realized that there really was no reason for me to worry about impressing this person. My job, in this case, was to be present, to hear what my inside voice was telling me, and to be my best possible self. My job, in all cases, is always the same. When I was able to reconnect with these truths, my worries and fears ceased and I entered the conversation more fully present. As the meeting ended, my potential new associate commented on my positive energy and personality. I smiled, knowing that what he saw, was what I heard. Not only had I gained a new associate, I had gained something much more. My balance had returned.

Janet M. Neal

The Ram Who Lost Her Focus

I THINK THAT THERE must be a mistake on my birth certificate. No, not my parents...way too many of the same personality traits to deny that one! And not the location – definitely Midwestern at heart. Possibly the year – most days I feel WAY younger than the age I'm supposed to be. No, it's the month. With the two distinct personalities that I've been experiencing of late, I swear that I must be a Gemini, the astrological sign of the Twins, and not an Aries, which boasts the sign of the Ram.

There is a side of me that is very much a go-getter. I get energized by doing more and more and love that adrenaline rush. There is nothing more satisfying than crossing something off my "To Do" list and moving on to the next task. I have taken great pride in being able to juggle many balls at the same time, and I love the start of something new. And then there's the other me...

This other side is the polar opposite. I am very content to putter around the house, doing little things here and there – or nothing at all. I could spend hours in bed and be content to never leave my house for days on end. A vacation at a beach with nothing to do but to read a good book is pretty close to heaven for me.

Having these two sides is fine as long as I can balance them and not let one or the other get too much control. If the energized side takes over I end up getting burned out and usually sick. If the sloth side wins, then pretty much nothing gets done and I start resenting my surroundings and the increasing demands on my time. I've learned over the years how to recognize when one side of me is getting a little too big for its britches and I take the steps to get things in check. Then there are those times when their battle for control causes a complete impasse and I have a minor meltdown. Yesterday was one of those days.

It's quite disturbing when I experience any type of conflict and it is especially so when the fight is focused inward. The part of me that wants to go, do, be organized and accomplished was in high gear, and the laid-back side just wanted to play and be loved. An image that came to me was of a person standing helplessly by the side of a highway, with life zooming past and around, wanting someone to slow down and notice them. The result was a feeling of complete frustration. The fix? Meditation! Seems I've kind of "forgotten" to take the time to quiet my mind and allow myself to decompress and ready myself for the day ahead.

Today's a new day and a new re-commitment to myself to get back on the beam with some necessary self-care. Maybe I'll find, after a time, that I'm really not a Gemini after all. Maybe I'm just a Ram who sometimes loses her focus. I'm looking forward to seeing "clearly" again!

An Alchemist at Heart

I THINK THAT, IN a past life, I must have been a scientist or an alchemist because, for most of this life, I have been searching for the magic formula – for just about everything. I try to figure out just what I can and can't eat in order to lose weight, what to do to feel better, what to wear to look better; it all has a certain complexity to it so that too much of this, or too little of that, will throw the whole thing off. No wonder I often feel exhausted!

This self-awareness came to mind the other day when I was recounting my story of "how I got here" to a new client at work. I was reflecting on my early days in the field of work/life balance and how it had grabbed me – so much more than my "real" job of selling computers. Now I see why: it has all those formulation elements!

I'm realizing that, at times, in order to feel balanced, I need to be in my head and actually figure out the numbers, like, "You can't work on that project until midnight tonight because YES, you do need seven hours of sleep." I need to actually write out a schedule, being the visual person that I am, so that I can see where my breaks will allow me to take a few moments for myself, or else my body is in a perpetual state of panic. And then, once I have "figured it out," I need to let go, and give control back to my heart, and trust that it's all good, regardless of what actually happens in the course of the day.

And now, according to my plans and calculations, one more swallow of coffee, a trip to the gym, and my day will be launched, in balance.

Authentic Living

I DID IT – I stopped coloring my hair. This decision was not something that my family was entirely excited about. But I had lived all of my 50+ years and I was willing to show the world just that. In fact, I loved my new look!

It sure was not always that way. How often did I try to look a certain way to please whomever I was with or, more likely, act according to what I thought that they would want? I scoured *Seventeen* magazines as a teen to find the perfect look, watched the other dancers at discos to get the right moves, and dyed my hair to hide my distinctive silver streak to garner a look more befitting for a young(ish) bride. I became a master chameleon.

But there was always this nagging feeling that this person was not the real me. That I was buried way down under the societal layers I had been amassing. I truly was feeling off, feeling out of balance. It was only when I was able to stop needing outside approval that I could start to listen to that voice inside of me. I was able to start honoring myself and my values, regardless of what others might be thinking.

Getting into balance is much more than an issue of time management. It is really getting myself re-aligned with my values. It is learning to be authentic and to hear that small voice inside. I needed to learn how to send my internal censor on a holiday and be willing to acknowledge any thought or feeling that surfaced. And each time I did this, I found it easier to do than the time before and wonderfully rewarding.

My journey toward balance certainly has been a process. I realized that, until I could fully incorporate all my values into my life, until I could celebrate my uniqueness and the gifts that my individuality could contribute to this world, and until I could embrace my own beauty within, I always would be out of balance, still searching for that ever elusive state.

As I look in the mirror now, I say a little welcome to the new, old me. I'm glad she's back!

Life in a Fog

ON MARTHA'S VINEYARD, WHERE I happily spent weeks of my summer vacation, the fog blows in and out frequently, if not regularly. You never know when it will arrive or how long it will last: a few minutes, hours or the entire day. But it does lift, eventually, in a period of time known only to a greater power than I.

There was a time when I would curse the fog, wanting it to hurry up and dissipate. Or be wary of it, of what it was obscuring. But I have learned to turn my thinking around about it. Instead, it creates a wrapped surprise. I can't wait to see what the day will be like when it lifts. It offers me not only the prospect of greater things ahead, but a chance to slow down now and concentrate, not on that which I can't see, but on that which I can – those things closest to me.

Our lives are often shrouded in a fog-like state. We can't see where we are going, or what is coming toward us. Many times that blanket creates a sense of panic and an unreasonable fear that this temporary state will, somehow, be everlasting. We flail around, searching for the quick fix, wanting to change our environment – now! But think about what happens when you are driving in fog at night and you decide to turn on your bright lights, hoping to better illuminate your path and speed your journey. The result is that you merely compound the blinding situation, as more water droplets reflect in your intense headlights. Sometimes, taking it easy, slowing down and using your low lights, or waiting for the fog to lift, are the only safe and reasonable solutions.

Consider the plight of a pilot who suddenly finds herself in a dense cloud cover. If she were to rely on her usual visual skills, she would be hard-pressed to find her way. And waiting it out while in flight might not be the smartest idea either!

What pilots do is rely on alternative information sources to assist them in navigating through dense clouds and fog. This technique is not something that comes naturally to most, but must be learned and practiced so that it becomes effective when needed.

And so it is with my life. When I find myself in a fog, I have several options, depending upon my attitude and my level of preparation. I can bemoan my fate. I could even cower in fear of the unseen and unknown. Or, I could choose to fight through it by using the tools that I have to help me. I can decide if waiting it out is an option. I can look forward with gleeful anticipation to what will be revealed when the fog lifts. I can use the cloud as a time of contemplation and reflection of that which is closest to me. And I can use alternative information sources to help me through: a trusted friend, a counselor, meditation, yoga or prayer.

Start using your alternative tools now, in your fog-less state, and you'll be amazed how much more effective they will be when you really need them. And remember, behind the clouds the sun is always shining!

On Becoming a Somebody

ROBERT REDFORD TURNED 75 a few weeks ago. That fact is up there near the top of the, "I can't believe it!" list, along with the weird weather and other strange earth rumblings of late. I do admit to having had a bit of a crush on the man in the past, but then again, who hasn't? That gorgeous face, that quiet strength...ahhh. He can't possibly be 75!

One of my favorite Redford movies is "The Way We Were." There is a scene in the film where Hubbell (Redford) and JJ (his best friend, played by Bradford Dillman) are out sailing and they are talking about the best and worst years of their lives. They fondly remember some of the better times that each has had, and there is mention made of JJ's marriage to Carole Ann breaking up. And then JJ says a line that has struck a chord in me from the moment I heard it. It is something like: "Old Carole Ann? Sorry buddy. She wasn't much. It's not like losing somebody. Like losing Katie... "

I always wanted to be "a Katie" after that.

In 1973 when the movie came out, I was fully vested in being whomever I thought you'd want me to be. I was very good at it. I had a knack for reading a situation and acting accordingly. The thought of being like Barbra Streisand's character "Katie," who stood up for her beliefs, regardless of whether they were popular or not, was COMPLETELY foreign and nearly unfathomable to me. But there was something in me that resonated with that movie line, as if a long-suppressed, authentic self finally saw a glimmer of hope that someday it could shine.

It may have taken decades for that light to emerge, but I think that it's pretty much what you see today. The other day there was one of those silly status updates on Facebook where you had to take the third letter of your last name and, using that letter, come up with a word to describe the person who had posted the status. Being a bit bored, and admittedly, curious, I played along. I cannot tell you how happy I was when someone posted the word "Real" to describe me. I really felt like a "somebody." I still like it when people agree with me, but gone is the need for that approval. Being a "somebody" to me is finding my path and taking it, no matter how twisted or turned it may be.

I would add my own word, if I could, to that listing of words to describe me: Aligned. I used to think that I was a balanced person, but now I'm realizing that it's more about alignment than anything else: alignment with my values, alignment with what I enjoy and alignment with what I want to do and be. What a fabulous way to live your life!

In "The Way We Were," Hubbell and Katie have an argument over her politics and his friends. He states, "People are more important than their principles." Katie replies, "People ARE their principles." I think I'm with Katie on this one. Or, at least I'm proud to say that Katie's way is the way I choose to live my life today. I'm awfully glad that the old "chameleon Janet" is just part of "the way I was." And I'd still welcome the opportunity to gently push the hair out of Robert Redford's eyes any day...

Soul in Control

I saw this quote on Facebook yesterday and although I'm not sure of the source, it really spoke to what I was thinking about:

Why do we close our eyes when we dream? When we cry? When we pray? Or when we kiss? Because we know that the most beautiful things in life are not seen, but felt by the heart.

I was closing my eyes in meditation when nearly the same idea came to me. I was reflecting on the noisiness of my mind, which then made me start to think about the brain. What an amazing organ! It is so powerful in directing how our bodies function, how we react, how we problem-solve, how we become creative. And yet, so often because it IS so powerful, we tend to think that the brain is what controls us. We relinquish our power to our mind.

The truth is that the mind is really like an amazing supercomputer. It not only takes in information and processes it like an ordinary computer, but it also has the remarkable ability to reason. Scientists continue to try to duplicate the brain's wondrous functions, but they haven't yet figured out that last piece.

I am grateful to have a strong mind; one that is both creative and practical in its thinking. Sure, some of those synapses have seen better days, but others continue to be created, as I learn and grow daily. And often, I judge myself on how effectively my mind is operating. Unfortunately, working from this perspective can not only set me up for disappointment and frustration, it can set in motion a negative spiral. Additionally, for most of my life – until very recently, actually – I felt that my mind was a gift that I was given and therefore I needed to use it to guide my life. I was wrong. Although yes, a strong mind is an amazing gift, and yes, I am truly grateful for it, the truth is that it is a TOOL, not the oracle of truth. My brain is a magnificent machine, guiding my body and actions and carrying out what, in my opinion, needs to be done. It is an amazing supercomputer of sorts and I have been allowing it to rule my life. But my brain is not the holder of the TRUTH. That would be my Soul. The Soul is the part of me that is eternal, that exists with or without this human vessel in which it currently resides. It is ageless and without constraints of time and space. It knows reality because it IS reality. And when I can shift my inner compass to have <u>it</u> , not my mind, be my guiding force, life flows. Pressures cease because they are external. Guilt and worry are not words in the Soul's vocabulary. Neither are the external trappings of society – these are concerns of the mind. The Soul is concerned about this moment, this precious second of being aware. And when I allow my Soul to be in control and I can exist within the here and now, there is nothing but peace and love. It is. Period.

I've also been thinking of the other things that I have come to know as being true. Here are a few:

- **You can't do it alone.** I am a master at convincing myself that I don't need any help, thank you very much. I am a fully capable individual who can handle whatever life gives me. In a LOT of cases, that statement holds true. But sometimes life gives you circumstances to show you that you <u>need</u> to reach out. Pride and denial are HUGE blocks to growth. Admitting when you are powerless, when you don't know it all, when you can dare to be vulnerable (yikes!), is the first step to letting in greater serenity and awareness.

+ **The answers are within**. Although for most of my life I looked to others to gauge how I was doing (did they like me, laugh at my jokes, tell me I was pretty, tell me I was smart, tell me I was doing the right thing, etc.), I never felt it was ENOUGH. I kept looking for more and more outside approval and still never felt complete. It wasn't until I could trust my own feelings and intuition that I truly was able to regain that serenity and "ahhhhh" feeling of being comfortable in my own skin.

+ **Feelings pass**. This seems so obvious and yet that reality totally escaped me for a large portion of my life. Because I felt so deeply, it was scary to be in the midst of certain feelings. And I really thought that if I got angry, I'd stay angry. Depressed? It would last forever. Happy I could deal with – in fact, I became a "happy junkie" in order to keep negative feelings at bay. There are all sorts of ways to keep unpleasant feelings away. I am sure that you can think of a few. But the truth is, it is OK to feel all of your feelings because the only way to get through them IS to go THROUGH them! I now think of them as clouds: sometimes they are dark and stormy, sometimes they are bouncy and playful and sometimes there are none at all, but in each case, they never stay that way forever. "This, too, shall pass," is an important phrase to remember.

+ **The answers come to you when you are quiet.** I get the most amazing insights when I am in the shower. I know it is because I am not rushing around, I am being distracted by what is going on around me, and I am not trying to think myself out of a situation. I am just allowing myself to be. Meditation has a similar affect: it is quieting yourself down with no expectations of anything and allowing whatever happens to happen. Sometimes nothing does, sometimes you sleep, and sometimes life becomes crystal clear. It is, at those times, that you realize that the answers are all there – it is the noise we create that distracts us from the truth.

+ **You can't fill a God-sized hole with anything else.** I had an empty feeling for years and felt that something was missing. Like there was a hole inside of me, almost an aching for something more. I tried various things to fill it up, including being very busy, eating a lot, drinking, spending money, relationships, etc. Although all of the above did work for a time, they were always temporary fixes and eventually they became ineffective, leaving me feeling worse. It wasn't until I realized that what I was missing was a spiritual connection to something greater than myself that I finally felt complete. Who knows what that "thing" is: call it God, the Universe, Spirit, Buddha, whatever – it is that power greater than myself that is in charge. I am not it. And releasing that burden that I had put on my shoulders, of feeling that I was in charge and therefore had to have all the answers, was incredible. I had a "partner" in whom I could trust, to whom I could go for advice and counsel and sympathy and love – at anytime, anywhere, in any situation. What an amazing feeling! My "God-size" amorphous hole is now filled and I am complete.

So when I get flooded with an overflowing list of "to dos" and expectations, placed on me by outside influences and my own doing, I'll try to breathe and recite the mantra, "My Soul is in control." And when I feel a slight upturning at the corners of my mouth, I'll know that it truly is!

About the Author

Janet Neal is passionate about living a balanced life because, well, she doesn't have much of a choice! As a single mother of three independent souls, an entrepreneur, a writer, coach, speaker and friend to many, Janet faces daily the same joys and frustrations as experienced by her readers. She not only brings her eclectic life experience and passion for living to her writings, but offers her readers solutions and inspiration as well.

Janet has been writing her newsletter and blog, *A Balanced Perspective*, since 2002, when she left her corporate life behind and entered the world of entrepreneurship. She has been a columnist in regional publications, quoted in numerous mainstream media, and has read her pieces on *Writing from the Heart* on Sirius Radio.

Janet lives happily in New Jersey (a place she said she'd never live) with her children and two dogs. You can visit her website at www.janetmneal.com.

Acknowledgements

I used to subscribe to the belief that was summed up in the Simon & Garfunkel song "I am a Rock": I am a rock. I am an island. We know how that worked out. Now I am embracing the philosophy of "It Takes a Village". And what a village I have to help me! Here are but a few:

TaRessa Stovall for listening to me and hearing my book title in my story.

Leanne Cesario and Peggy Menaker for their kind and tireless reading...and attention to details that sometimes (often) allude me.

Deborah Dunn for her unrelenting nudging to actually bring this dream to reality.

Mary-Faith Marriott for her insistence that we keep writing, no matter what.

Nancy Aronie, who created the safe place to allow the writer in me to flourish.

Julie Maloney and Jacqueline Sheehan who do the same in their amazing writing retreats.

Cynthia Arias and her team (Felix, Leonard & Sefu) at Freedom Triumphs who believe in my vision and helped bring it to the internet.

Marie Lourdes for her beautiful book cover design.

Kim, Melanie, Leanne, Elizabeth, Whitney, Filomena and Liz – who know me oh so well and keep pushing me onward.

Nancy Just, who has heard more stories from me than any one person should ever have to hear…and still sticks around for more!

The University of Santa Monica – where I learned that the impossible can truly become possible.

The members of The Professional Women's Center who believed in me and my vision.

My innumerable friends, colleagues and acquaintances – each interaction fills me with inspiration and gratitude.

And finally,

My In-Laws, Maureen Neal and the late Richard Neal – what a gift to be loved for being me!

My sisters Jean and Joan MacMeekin – for putting up with me as a big sister

My parents, Barbara and John MacMeekin – for believing in me. Always.

My fiancé, Jim Savage – for being my biggest cheerleader

And my beautiful children, Timothy, Christopher and Emily – the gifts that keep on giving!!